# Tender Loving Fun

## *A Guide to Adult Babysitting*

# by

# Sam McCue

First Published 2022

Copyright © AB Discovery 2022

All rights reserved.

No part of this publication may be reproduced, stored in a retrieval system, transmitted in any form, by any means electronic, mechanical, photocopying, recording, or otherwise without the prior written permission of the publisher and author.

Any resemblance to any person, either living or dead, or actual events are a coincidence.

Title: Tender Loving Fun

Author: Sam McCue

Editors: Michael and Rosalie Bent

Publisher: AB Discovery

© 2022

www.abdiscovery.com.au

**Other Books by Sam McCue**

The Candy Stripers

The Nannies

Baby Governor

Sitter Search

This and other books are also available in audiobook format.

# Contents

# 1. | What Is Infantilism?

Ⅰf you've opened this book, you're at least open-minded to the notion of caring for an adult baby. Here you'll find more information on regression, learn what you'll be taking on if you decide to try the caregiver role, and become familiar with the nominal skills required for the unique job of 'big' babysitting.

As an adult, you have probably enjoyed some form of regressive activity yourself ... something childlike or babyish that helps you relieve stress, unwind from a long day, or calms and soothes you. You might have a stuffed animal on your bed, enjoy watching a favorite cartoon from your childhood, or like taking a long bubble bath.

Adult babies take this sort of behavior to an extreme. For an adult baby, there's nothing more sublime, peaceful, or calming than regressing to the state of a baby or small child. For someone like you who chooses to care for an adult baby, the experience can be just as emotionally fulfilling and even transformative.

So, what is an adult baby? An adult baby indulges in something psychologists call *infantilism*. Essentially, adult babies are post-pubescent individuals seeking the emotional experience of returning to childhood or infancy. To make this journey back in time, they use various regression techniques and items like baby bottles, baby food, bibs, and diapers to recreate an authentic experience.

However, the psychologist's term, 'infantilism' is old-fashioned and tends to be a misleading label for the worldwide adult baby community. While some infantilists do want to regress to actual *infancy*, the vast majority regress to something approaching *toddlers*. While the term 'adult baby' is in common use, 'adult toddler' would be far more accurate.

Most infantilists prefer the term 'Little One,' which is an identifier I'll use often throughout the book. This term implies that infantilists enjoy being 'little' but specifying a target age or gender. Nor does it imply a sexual drive or any dysfunctional aspects. Adults in the regressive scenario are commonly referred to as 'Bigs' perhaps more precisely identified as 'Nanny', 'Mommy' or 'Daddy'.

Little Ones are not *dysfunctional*. They do, however, have a sometimes-overpowering drive – a genuine *need* to be babied – that *can* cause them problems. But then again, who *doesn't* have a drive or need deep inside that causes them occasional problems? When these needs and drives overwhelm or consume an adult to an unmanageable extent, dysfunction generally comes into play.

That's where you come in.

You can help a Little One avoid any sort of visible dysfunction by recreating a time when they were unconditionally loved and cared for. In essence, you can help an adult escape being an adult … even if for just a few hours. Who among us wouldn't enjoy that?

Many Little Ones are highly intelligent, effective people, who conduct business, have an active social life, and manage complex interpersonal relationships with a high degree of success. Tucked away in their kitchen cabinets, however, are baby bottles, bibs, and jars of baby food. At night, these Little Ones may wet the bed or wear diapers. In their closets may hang adult-sized baby clothes. They may have and use a crib, highchair and have toys and other baby things hidden away from prying eyes.

While these people are *not* dysfunctional with respect to how they work, behave, and interact with others, they are very *different.*

Society has a common and disturbing habit of expecting everyone to conform to a common set of ideals and behaviors, while still proclaiming that each of us has a right to individuality. In a general sense, this is a good thing, as it brings a unity of purpose and a cohesive society. However, if conformity is taken too far, individuality suffers and those who don't fit neatly into society's pre-formed little boxes begin to suffer. Little Ones obviously do not fit into society's pre-cut definitions of *normal.*

The modern era has seen many previously marginalized groups integrated into society. Adult Babies and Little Ones are, however, not among them. Society is still in the process of discovering that they exist. All this sounds easy enough to grasp, but explanations cannot describe the inner turmoil experienced by many adult babies. Most Little Ones still struggle with the impact of regression and the deep need to be a child again ... if only for a brief period.

*How did this happen to them, and why can't they let it go?*

For most people, the simple truth is that we don't know. To determine why regression is part of the personality is a long and complex procedure that, even when it is successful, rarely offers much in the way of resolution. Through patient, compassionate and openminded caregiving, however, you can offer invaluable assistance to a Little One. Best of all, you will likely find the experience both fun and fulfilling. Regression is all about comfort and need, and you can provide care that fulfills both. In the process, you may find that you are fulfilling a deeply parental need for yourself.

Any number of triggers can instill a regressive nature into a child. The obvious triggers are severe trauma or physical abuse of some sort. Clear and obvious experiences like these always have a strong impact on the development of the child, but it is also true that the trauma may be a *perceived* one, as much as an actual occurrence. A child that *perceives* he or she is not getting enough nurturing from a mother or father can sometimes feel traumatized. Consequently, some Little Ones may develop a strong need for regressive nurturing later in life, even though the parenting may have been quite adequate. In my own case, for example, my parents did a wonderful job.

Some Little Ones claim that their childhood history of extensive bedwetting initiated their regressive needs. While they disliked the bedwetting, they also grew to attach deeply regressive feelings toward the bedtime ritual involved. Eventually, it became a part of their own regression or escape back to childhood, despite finding it unpleasant and uncomfortable.

This brings us to a fundamental truth:

---

*Triggers and objects in regression may not always be pleasant ones. Some may be harsh and unpleasant feelings and memories, yet they can still trigger regression. An old-fashioned pin-on diaper, for example, may evoke painful or humiliating memories, yet still forms a large part of the regressive experience.*

---

Rosalie Bent's excellent *There's Still A Baby in My Bed!* cites an example of one girl who grew up to discover that her need to regress was actually motivated, to some extent, by her mother's well-intentioned efforts to stop her.

*"I've been an adult baby since I <u>was</u> a baby! Sound confusing? Well, I first remember doing dress-up in the attic when*

I was about six. Oh, I did the mommy dress-up, wearing her clothes and shoes, but I always gravitated to the box of my old diapers and baby things.

As soon as my parents told me that I couldn't act like a baby anymore, I knew they were wrong. Surely they thought I was potty trained, but I would spend hours in the attic doing dress-up in more than just mom's things. I loved putting on diapers and just being a baby.

When I was eleven years old, my mom caught me. She was never one for being comfortable with things that weren't clearly defined by the Protestant church. Her prepubescent daughter padding around in cloth diapers was not something her minister would have an answer for. She immediately preached to me that I was not a baby anymore, that this was sick, and by the way, I was grounded. It would have been so much nicer if she had just pulled my diapers down and spanked me. Of course, I don't think she would have had any intention to pull the diapers back up!

The next day, my boxes of baby things in the attic were gone.

I was frightened, angry, and confused. I sucked my thumb for another year or so. They couldn't take that away from me, although my blankie mysteriously kept getting smaller. I got even, though. I was a raging hormone-mad girl. It had to be their three toughest years of raising me. No matter what, they were wrong, even when they were right.

I kept that longing of being a baby suppressed for a long, long time. I was never able to get past the ingrained guilt. It wasn't until fifteen years ago or so, that I actually allowed myself to try on a disposable diaper. It was as if someone had flipped a switch. I felt so calm, complacent, and comfortable. I started 'doing the research' to find an incredible adult baby community, it was huge! I loved what I found. I wore diapers for thirty days straight. I kept denying that I was a baby, yet I would pick up toys, baby bottles, sippy cups, and pacifiers when I was out shopping."

Obviously, the sort of dress-up and role-playing this young woman describes are solitary pursuits. However, they harm no one and provide her with calming relief from the stress and anxiety of being an adult. For many Little Ones, the next step in the evolutionary process is finding a caregiver to help or guide them through a regressive episode. Of course, many still remember babysitters who cared for them when they were actual children. This is the sort of interaction they are striving to recreate. As a caregiver for an adult baby, you assume the role of a babysitter. Essentially, you become the temporary parent of a regressive adult.

If you yourself babysat as a pre-teen or teenager, or if you are a parent, you can probably recall dozens or hundreds of caregiving experiences. When you babysit a big baby, you provide the same care and concern that you'd provide for a toddler, even though the 'baby' at the center of the experience is perfectly capable of caring for themselves.

In some ways, caring for a regressed Little One is much easier than caring for a real child. For example, Little Ones seldom actually hurt themselves, and you don't have to be constantly vigilant or always worried about the baby's safety. While some adult babies do cry when they're upset or needy, most can communicate quite easily... even if they just point to something they want. The communication hurdles you typically encounter with a small child don't exist with most Little Ones.

I tend to take pride in being an *activist* adult baby. Over the past 40 years, I've had 20 or so babysitters. Many have told me that the care they provided me was identical to the care they'd have given a real baby, with one key difference: **Everything is bigger**. Almost without exception, they've all enjoyed caring for me, and most have had so much fun babysitting me that they couldn't wait to do it again.

If you're a caregiver, a healthcare professional, or an experienced babysitter, nothing about caring for an adult baby should surprise or challenge you. You'll need to know – or need to learn – how to do a half-dozen things well:

- Undress and dress your Little One

- Give a bath

- Feed a bottle, baby food, or toddler-type finger food

- Change a diaper

- Help your 'big baby' play effectively

- Put your Little One down for a nap

Having had a score of babysitters, I have noticed that no two caregivers ever manage these tasks in the same way. The challenge is to view caring for a big baby for what it is: An opportunity for your individual creativity to take center stage. Don't be afraid to improvise or adapt what you're doing to fit changing environments and circumstances.

Similarly, it's hard to make a mistake when caring for a Little One. The world won't stop if you drop a pacifier on the floor or can't find a much-loved stuffed toy. There are only a half-dozen cardinal rules to keep in mind:

**First, you're in charge.** Your Little One may want to test boundaries, as a real toddler or small child would. I like to think that's why God invented time-outs. However, as much as all of us think we'd enjoy being the boss, there are some caveats that come along with being in charge. For example:

**Second, you'll need a plan.** Many adult babies are easily bored, but because of their regressive mindset, they often don't want to be asked what they want to do next. For a neophyte caregiver, this is hard to avoid. Whether you're babysitting for an hour or a weekend, you should have a plan or sequence of events in mind before you start.

You can begin your time together by undressing and dressing your Little One, or you may want to walk in and find a fully dressed big baby waiting for you. While some babysitters believe that undressing and dressing their charge helps reinforce the notion that they're running the show, others prefer to avoid the 'adult' in the adult baby entirely. The choice is yours.

If you've never cared for a chronological adult, you may find it difficult to imagine a fully grown person wearing diapers and baby clothes. For that reason, you may wish to explore the idea of a 'mechanical' babysitting session first, so you have some time to become accustomed to the more perfunctory aspects of caregiving without the regression component in play. I'll talk more about 'mechanical sessions' later in this book.

**Third, you're there to care.** Unlike the stereotypical teenaged babysitter, you should probably stay off your cellphone and focus on your Little One... even during nap time. As I've mentioned, many adult babies are easily bored and can become incredibly anxious if the caregiver is off doing something else.

The Little One you babysit may have a crib, highchair, playpen, and changing table ... or nothing babyish at all beyond ordinary furniture. I've come to believe that adult cribs and scaled-up baby furniture are only props. You can change a big baby's diaper while they lie on the floor or on their bed, put them to bed wherever they usually sleep and sit them down on a barstool or at the dining table to feed them. Most of the time, I'm fed a bottle while I'm lying on the sofa. The sofa is just the most comfortable place, but it's not particularly babyish!

For this reason, you may find that you are more comfortable asking your Little One to pack a diaper bag and come to you rather than going to their place. Since you're in charge, the choice of the venue is yours to make. Many 'professional' babysitters acquire the furniture they need – an adult-sized crib, highchair, changing table, and so on – and use the same nursery furnishings to care for several different Little Ones on a continuing basis. Of course, all the 'props' represent quite an investment, which helps explain why 'professional' big babysitters charge steep fees for their time.

If you choose to go to the Little One's house or apartment, you'll certainly need to familiarize yourself with the layout, but that typically takes only a few minutes. The rest of the time should be spent with your big baby. Sit beside your Little One when you put them down for a nap or sit on the floor and help them play. While I have had babysitters browse my bookshelves or watch TV while I played or napped, the best ones stayed with me most of the time. My infantilism stems from deeply rooted abandonment issues, and the regressed toddler I become is often frightened if I'm left alone.

**Fourth, you can always take a time-out.** Of course, this is something you can't do with an actual baby, but the Little One will understand if you need a 5-minute or 10-minute break. Actually, some convenient break times are already built into a babysitting session:

- While the Little One is napping
- While the Little One is soaking in the bathtub
- While the Little One is playing or watching TV

Sometimes, adult babies can be demanding enough that you need to step outside just to get back to the real world. Take a few minutes to go out and listen to the birds singing, see the sun shining, or just feel the breeze. This will often help you recharge the babysitter batteries enough to continue on.

A fully regressed Little One will likely not understand why you'd request a time-out, so you'll probably need to look for opportunities to make your own rather than ask for it. A Little One who has not regressed, on the other hand, will be able to help you solve whatever issue has arisen so the session can continue.

Assuming you're being paid to babysit, and not caring for a Little One out of the goodness of your heart, you should use time-outs sparingly. However, unlike 'real' babysitting, time-outs can help you recover your sanity when you're trying to handle a particularly demanding adult baby.

**Fifth, focus on continuous improvement.** Once the first-time jitters are out of the way, think about how you'll improve your interactions with your Little One. Every babysitting session should get better. There's always something you can work on and make easier, more realistic, or more fun.

For most inexperienced adult babysitters, there's always one key area of improvement to focus on: *Communication*. Most adults find it hard to 'relate' to another adult as if they were talking with a child. For some babysitters, talking to an adult baby as if they *are* a baby can be embarrassing and extraordinarily difficult.

Years ago, one of my babysitters was a former United States Marine. Her boot camp experiences were traumatic and degrading. One day, she walked past the officers' quarters and saw her Sergeant and other instructors yelling at boxes on the floor! This young woman needed a few moments to realize that her drill instructor and the others were *practicing*. If you think you'll need help to talk to an adult as you'd talk to a baby, practice! I can be somewhat intimidating as an adult, so this young woman practiced for her interactions with me by talking to a stuffed toy.

Of course, there's no need to constantly baby-talk an adult baby. However, there is a very real need to keep the communication at the level a toddler can understand. When the 'toddler' in front of you is a fully functioning adult, this can be a challenge. Communication issues can usually be easily handled with the right mindset.

*Keep one rule of thumb in mind: If you wouldn't say it to a two-year-old, don't say it to a regressed Little One.*

The list of activities that require practice to master is quite long. For example, it's often a challenge to securely fasten an adult diaper. The consequences of failing to do so can be little short of disastrous, so this is a skill that is best learned quickly. For this reason, I've provided entire chapters on each challenge ... naps and playtime, dressing, and so on.

**Sixth, enjoy yourself!** I don't want to overstate the challenge of the learning hurdles I've mentioned. Babysitting an adult is relatively simple work, and the fact is that most adult babies are yearning for the sort of care you can provide them. Even if your time together is not perfect, your Little One will likely enjoy the time together immensely. That sort of positive experience is enhanced if you can share their joy as your own.

If you've never cared for an adult in any other context – and especially if you have – you may find yourself wondering how you'll enjoy tasks like diapering and feeding. This is where the communication mindset I've already discussed pays big dividends. Changing a diaper or feeding a jar of strained bananas is much easier if you *see* the Little One you're caring for as a *toddler* rather than as an *adult.*

The key point to remember is that the few unpleasant tasks involved in big baby care are over and done with quite quickly, leaving you free to return to playtime or another part of the babysitting routine that you enjoy.

At this point, you probably have two questions: *What is the actual experience of all this really like, and can I do it?* I can assure you that the answer to the second question is an emphatic 'yes!'

To get a sense of the actual experience – and to try to get your head around the notion of *babysitting* a healthy adult – I've chosen to relate one of my favorite babysitter's 'first time' sessions in the chapter that follows.

# 2. | A Babysitting Session

The summer of 2007 was a challenging time for me because I found myself with no real recourse for my babying needs. I decided to run a brief 'help wanted' ad on one of the local internet message boards:

*ISO Nursing Student, Nanny, or Frustrated Actress*

*Healthy middle-aged male seeks part-time caregiver for unusual work.*

*Nothing illegal, immoral, or fattening! Applicants should be young at heart, physically fit, and have a good deal of childcare or healthcare experience.*

*Hourly rate of pay dependent on skill and personality.*

*Respond with your favorite color in the subject line to weed out the buckets of spam I usually get, and tell me a little about yourself and your background or training.*

*Thanks for your time! I look forward to hearing from you.*


I received a reply that evening from a young lady named Zoey Morton. Zoey was 28 at the time, and she'd graduated from a nearby high school. She'd spent some time at a nearby community college, worked a broad range of healthcare jobs, and was currently nannying two small boys three days a week. She needed work on the other two days.

I emailed Zoey back. Sensing that she was a good candidate, I explained that I am an infantilist and that I find comfort and relaxation in being 'babysat' for brief periods of time. In the email, I mentioned that I was a professional and well-known in the community and that I expected absolute discretion.

I gave Zoey no more background or information than that. I did mention that I could give her one afternoon of work per week for the next several months and that I was prepared to pay $25 per hour. I suggested that we meet for coffee at a local restaurant later that week.

Zoey agreed, and – without my asking – sent me back a photo of herself. A leggy brunette, she wore glasses, had long wavy hair, and seemed attractive and unassuming. We met for coffee, wound up talking for a couple of hours about what she'd done and where she was heading with her life and then, by process of elimination, talked about my infantilism.

"So," Zoey asked rather plainly, "do you wear diapers?"

I told Zoey that I did. She said that diapering wasn't a problem for her. She'd been changing babies – and not a few older adults – for a decade. But her next question shocked me: She wanted to know what *kind* of diapers I wore. When I told her, she wanted to know the manufacturer.

Zoey, as it turned out, was quite the earth mother type. She seemed genuinely pleased when I told her that I wore cloth diapers. She'd recommended the same manufacturer's diapers to a family with whom she worked. At the time, however, Zoey's response was unusual. Most babysitters I'd recruited were far more comfortable with Pampers and the like than they were with the cloth diapers my generation had worn.

Quite apart from her warm attitude toward cloth diapering, I liked Zoey immediately. She was quiet, seemed studious, and assured me several times that caring for me would pose no problems for her. She obviously wanted the job. My next open afternoon was that Thursday. I suggested Zoey let me take her to lunch and then I would show her where I lived. We could go from there.

After a pleasant lunch on Thursday, I drove home, and Zoey followed me. She had a tiny Honda that seemed about to fall apart. I walked her through the large home and finally showed her my nursery. She pulled up the drop side on my Winnie the Pooh crib, tugged the big tray off my wooden highchair, and flipped through the oversized onesies and baby clothing in the closet. Finally, she walked to my changing table, picked up one of the snap-on cloth diapers, and studied it with interest.

Zoey walked across the room to our small loveseat, smoothed her skirt behind her and sat down. "I certainly want the job," she told me, "But I'm a bit unsure that I can treat you like a little boy."

"That will take some practice," I told her. I was still standing in the doorway. "Please don't worry about it," I added. I watched Zoey continue to fidget with her skirt.

"Would you like to try?" I finally asked. "We can make a start this afternoon if you're comfortable. Maybe you could give me a bath."

Rather than just telling Zoey what I wanted her to do, I made a suggestion, because she seemed the type of young woman who didn't appreciate being ordered about.

"A bath would be great," Zoey said and stood up. She headed toward the bathroom, asking me if we had bubble bath. Satisfied with what I usually had on hand, Zoey turned the taps and began filling the bathtub. I walked into my bedroom, sat on the bed, and started removing my clothing.

A moment later, Zoey was in my doorway. "Do you need any help?" she asked. She was obviously trying to be accommodating, and I sensed that she was struggling to interact with me as she would have talked to one of the little boys she nannied. I stripped to my underwear and followed Zoey back down the hallway to the bathroom. I stood on the little bath rug while Zoey sat down on the edge of the bathtub, added the bubble bath, and tested the water. She beckoned me to her, and then she whisked my underwear down to my feet. Her interest in my naked body seemed nonexistent.

Zoey turned off the taps and waited while I settled into the tub. Convinced that I wasn't going to drown myself, she told me she wanted to find some clothes for me to wear and left me to soak for a few minutes. I knew she was trying to get the measure of the strange house and my nursery, and I was honestly grateful for the brief time alone.

Zoey returned to find me still sitting in bubbles, my eyes closed. She sat back down on the side of the tub, dipped the little ducky bath mitt into the warm water, and then squirted some baby wash into the wet terrycloth. She began bathing me, scrubbing vigorously across my shoulders and then down my arms. She finished my back and chest, then moved to my thighs, legs, and feet. By that point, the bubbles had abated a bit.

"Do you want to wash your private area yourself?" Zoey asked. I wasn't sure why she'd asked, but she was obviously trying to protect what little modesty I had left. I just shook my head. She cleaned me gently but thoroughly, then rinsed me, pulled the drain, and helped me stand up. I stepped out of the bathtub. Using my big bath towel, Zoey dried me from the head down, then draped the damp towel over my head like a shawl. She took my hand and led me back down the hallway to my nursery.

I noticed that a few things there were out of kilter. My changing mat was lying on the floor, along with a different colored diaper, a diaper liner, and a jar of Vaseline. I'd been diapered and changed on the floor a hundred times or so by that point, and I knew some women liked using the floor rather than a changing table. For the first few times, at least, the floor had certain advantages.

Zoey gave my shoulders one last rub with the big bath towel, then pulled it off me. I sank down to my knees and lay on the changing mat. Then she was beside me, asking me to lift slightly so she could slide the diaper beneath me. She added the diaper liner and then opened the Vaseline. Her warm, slippery fingers spread the nursery jelly across my clean-shaven groin.

"I'm glad you're nice and smooth here," Zoey whispered. She closed the Vaseline, brought the front of the diaper up between my legs, and snapped the sides. I lay on the floor, eyes closed, while Zoey gathered up my Thomas the Tank Engine onesie and light blue booties.

"I know you'll look cute in this," she said. I sat up and let her tug the onesie over my head, then I lay back down so she could fish the long flap from beneath me and snap it closed. Zoey moved to my feet and pushed the booties on. I was still lying on the changing pad, and Zoey began rubbing my ankles in a sort of curious massage. I closed my eyes. What she was doing felt good and I was suddenly aware of feeling very tired. I often feel overwhelming fatigue as I'm regressing.

"Would you like a bottle?" Zoey asked. I opened my eyes and nodded. She got to her feet. "You just stay still," she told me. "I'll find them." She walked out of the room. I'd left an envelope on the kitchen counter, addressed 'Zoey'. In the envelope were five $20 bills. I'm not sure when Zoey spotted it, but the envelope was gone when she left that evening.

Zoey was out of the room for four or five minutes. I had enough time to sit up slightly, wet my pants, and then lie back down.

When Zoey came back, she held a glass baby bottle filled with apple juice. She grabbed a baby diaper from a stack on the changing table and sat down on the floor beside me, extending her long legs and arching her knees.

I didn't need instruction or encouragement. I crawled into Zoey's lap and settled against her breast. She wasn't particularly full-figured and cuddling with Zoey was no effort. I opened my mouth and let her pop the nipple in.

As I nursed, I noticed Zoey smelled fresh and clean ... like Ivory soap. She'd acquired her back-to-nature sensibility from her parents, who were both flower children of the 1960s. At once both elemental and feminine, Zoey wasn't fastidious about anything beyond her clothing. She didn't seem to mind me cuddling against her. I felt quite peaceful and contented.

As I worked the nipple, Zoey began gently stroking my eyebrows and hair. I slowed my nursing pace because I honestly didn't want the time to end. I still had an ounce or two of juice remaining in the bottle when I felt Zoey's right hand move down to my diaper. She gave the front of the onesie a gentle squeeze. Zoey reached down and carefully unsnapped the bottom of the onesie, then slipped her open palm inside the loose waistband of my diaper.

"You're wet like a boy," she said, in a self-satisfied sort of voice.

I remember being confused. "I *am* a boy," I thought to myself.

"Can you finish this on your own?" Zoey finally asked. She was still holding the bottle. I grasped the nurser with both hands, as a toddler might, and Zoey slid from beneath me. Still on her knees, she turned and pulled a clean diaper and a package of baby wipes from the changing table. Then she turned back to me.

"Move over to the changing pad, little boy," she said simply, and I did as I was told.

Zoey unsnapped the diaper and pulled down the wet front. "Good job," she said loudly. "We've got a nice wet diaper here." She seemed to be congratulating me for wetting my pants. I know now that Zoey was trying to relate to me as she would one of her charges. At the time, however, her enthusiasm took me by complete surprise. I've never had another babysitter tell me "Good job" for having a wet diaper.

I focused on finishing the bottle while Zoey changed my diaper. A few minutes later, she was snapping up my onesie when the last drops of juice drained through the nipple. The bottle gave that characteristic ringing sound that always heralds an empty nurser. Zoey rolled the wet diaper up but left it lying on the floor. She picked up the clean baby diaper and spread it across her shoulder. Then she helped me sit up and leaned me into her so she could burp me.

Zoey's rhythmic pats were so effective that I actually spit up a little juice into the burp cloth. The spit-up did not go unnoticed.

Zoey stood up. She picked up the wet diaper and the empty bottle. Dropping the burp cloth and the wet diaper into the diaper pail, she walked out of the room to take the nurser back to the kitchen. She was back in a moment, and I was still sitting on the floor.

"Why don't you show me how you climb into your crib?" the young woman suggested. I got up from the floor and walked over to the little step stool I used. I held her hand as I climbed into the baby bed. Once I was comfortable, Zoey covered me with the little crib blanket.

"Where's your Binky?" she asked. I remember finding it strange that she hadn't asked until then. I pointed at a NUK pacifier that sat atop the changing table. Zoey retrieved it, popped it into my mouth, and stood beside me for a few minutes, stroking my hair and fussing with the blanket. I finally closed my eyes, and I could hear Zoey sit down on the little loveseat. I didn't intend to fall asleep, but I did.

When I awoke, Zoey was sitting on the little loveseat, her bare feet tucked beneath her, reading one of my child-level books on pirates. I propped myself up on an elbow, the pacifier still in my mouth. The crib mattress supports creaked a bit, showing their age after several years of use.

Zoey looked up. "I was reading about Anne Bonny," she said. "She was younger than me when she disappeared. How are you doing, little boy?"

Zoey unfolded herself and walked over to the crib. She lowered the drop side, pulled down the crib blanket, and pushed a finger past the onesie and into one of the diaper leak guards. I felt her fingertip brush against me with a brief tickle. I expected the young woman to hustle me out of the crib, but she began unsnapping my onesie as I lay on my back. She left me for a moment to get a clean diaper and wipes from the changing table.

"I hope you haven't made too much of a mess," Zoey said softly as she unsnapped my diaper. "I don't want to change the crib, too. Let's see what you did."

She held the front of my diaper against me as if she expected me to squirt her, but she was in no real danger. Zoey made no further comment while she changed my wet diaper. She dropped the diaper into the diaper pail and returned to snap up my onesie.

"I saw that big roller coaster in the bottom of your closet," Zoey said while she was helping me from the crib. "My boyfriend loves K'Nex. I know we can't finish it today, but we can start it. Would you like that?"

Working on the carpet in my nursery, we made a start. The K'Nex roller coaster was several years old at that time, and I'd never opened it. The toy had been a Christmas gift from another babysitter. Zoey was quite chatty while we were working out the initial steps. She read the instruction manual aloud while she told me about her life. I know it sounds trite to say that we bonded over K'Nex, but that's the truth.

I learned about her boyfriend – Brandon – and his railroad job that kept him away from home for days at a time. Brandon lived in a Yurt and was apparently as concerned about the environment as Zoey. They'd been together, off and on, since junior high school.

Then Zoey told me about her family and parents … her siblings, what sort of jobs they had, and so on. We'd been working on the roller coaster for about 40 minutes when the young woman stopped her monologue.

"The one time I want to find out about someone," Zoey said, laughing, "and I'm the one doing all the talking." She reached over and pulled the NUK from my mouth, trying to facilitate some conversation on my part. I'm sure I just stared at her.

Zoey laughed again. "I guess that's okay," she said quietly. "How's that diaper holding up?"

In all the months she cared for me, Zoey never referred to diapers as anything else. I'd become accustomed to hearing my diaper called 'pants,' for example. Zoey never used any of the popular synonyms. Maybe she was afraid of confusing a little boy like me.

I was on my knees, and I turned toward her so she could do another diaper check. She replaced the NUK first.

"I think you can wait a little bit," Zoey said after she'd tickled me again with her long forefinger. "I can hear your tummy. There's baby food in the kitchen, right? I know I saw some."

I nodded. Zoey got up, smoothed her skirt, and walked out of the room.

I finished my K'Nex task, sat on the floor and waited. Zoey walked back in a few minutes later, carrying two jars of baby food, a baby spoon, and another bottle of juice. She sat everything down on the highchair tray, then slid the tray off the highchair. As acrobatic as that might sound, she did it easily. Nothing spilled.

"Let's get you up into your highchair," Zoey said, putting the tray down on the loveseat. She busied herself untying my bib, which had been hanging on the back of the highchair. I got up and climbed into the highchair.

Zoey bibbed me, slid on the highchair tray, and fed me a jar of chilled Gerber strained bananas, which – in certain circumstances – are quite wonderful. She fed me with a minimum of fuss and surprisingly little conversation, especially given the fact that she hadn't stopped talking during our playtime. I had a liberal quantity of strained bananas smeared across my chin when we finished the jar.

Without much preliminary, Zoey opened the second jar. Hawaiian Delight had something of a laxative effect on me. Zoey would later tell me that she would have appreciated some warning. That night, however, she just stirred the baby food and fed me the entire jar.

Zoey wiped my face, untied my bib, slid the tray off the highchair, and grabbed the nurser and a clean burp cloth from the stack on the changing table. She sat down on the far end of the loveseat and patted the cushion next to her. I sat down and leaned across her, bumping my head on the arm of the loveseat. I managed to adjust myself and Zoey popped the nipple of the bottle into my mouth.

I took about 15 minutes to finish the eight ounces of cold apple juice. I kept my eyes closed the entire time. Zoey kept stroking my hair and my cheek. She said not a word.

27

The bottle emptied with a sound better imagined than described. I kept the nipple in my mouth for a few moments, unwilling to let the time end. Finally, Zoey pulled the nipple from my mouth and helped me sit up. She tugged the burp cloth across her left shoulder and guided me onto her. She'd been patting my back for perhaps half a minute when I burped.

"Goodness!" Zoey exclaimed. She continued to burp me and said nothing more.

Satisfied, Zoey helped me out of her embrace. I stood and walked over to the changing pad on the floor, intent on continuing with the roller coaster construction. Zoey followed me, bent down, and picked up the pad. She put it back on the changing table, then patted the middle.

"I want you up here this time," Zoey said quietly. Thus far, she'd changed me on the floor and in my crib. She wanted this new venue because she suspected I was sitting on more than my juice.

Zoey popped the NUK back into my mouth and stood beside me for a moment, patting my thigh. She watched me carefully, waiting until I'd closed my eyes before she began unsnapping my onesie. She started humming to herself – the theme from the old Andy Griffith show – and then asked, "Do you like the Andy Griffith reruns? I like the episodes when the Darlings come down out of the hills." Briscoe Darling and his bucolic family had been infrequent guests in Mayberry.

With the pacifier in my mouth, I could not answer, and I didn't open my eyes. I lifted a bit so she could slide the back flap of my onesie beneath me, out of harm's way. Zoey unsnapped the diaper, then used the front and some baby wipes to get me clean.

At length, Zoey's humming ceased. The young woman gathered up the diaper and wipes and dropped the bundle into the diaper pail.

Zoey slid a clean diaper beneath me and reached for the large bottle of Baby Magic on the side of the changing table. She squirted some into her hand and began to rub it into my skin. "I love that smell," she said. I'd heard other women make the same comment.

I was glad to be in a clean diaper. I slid off the changing table and followed Zoey out of the nursery and down the hall to the living room. She sat on the sofa and patted the cushion. I sat down beside her.

I looked at the clock on the wall to my right. The time was nearly 7 o'clock. Zoey had been with me for almost five hours. At that point, I realized I must have slept an hour or so in my crib, which was an incredible accomplishment for an anxious insomniac like me. I was flatly astounded.

Zoey clicked the television remote, and we sat watching the last few minutes of some inane game show. We shifted through the credits and began watching a situation comedy. About 10 minutes into the show, Zoey patted my leg.

"Well, little boy," she said quietly, as she looked at my face. "I guess I should go. Are you going to be okay?"

Just then, I felt that familiar sensation – like a rubber band snapping against my skin – as I quickly returned to the real world. Zoey thought I was starting to cry. I hadn't felt so at ease with a babysitter in quite some time. Zoey reached out to hug me, and I found myself sliding back into her arms as if I'd never left her embrace.

"Can you come back on Tuesday?" I finally asked, my chin resting on her shoulder. Tuesday was her other day off from her usual nannying job.

"Of course," Zoey whispered in my ear. "We'll build more of the roller coaster. Send me an email and let me know how you think we did." With that, she stood up and smoothed her skirt yet again. Zoey retreated to the kitchen for her purse and headed to the front door.

"Don't stay up too late, baby," Zoey said as she closed the door behind her.

I finally heaved myself up from the sofa, walked to the door, and locked it. I walked back to the sofa, intent on finding something else on television.

# 3. | Setting the Stage

Different Little Ones derive different benefits from being babysat. I've never tried cocaine, but I imagine the euphoria I feel after being babied is something akin to a cocaine 'high'. I also look forward to getting a good night's sleep, which is usually a genuine rarity for me.

After being cared for, the contented feeling is much like the relaxation and contentment that follows a deep massage. Even though the aftereffects are fleeting and transitory – at least, they are in my case – the anticipation of that experience drives me to arrange another babysitting session … and another …

I am a 'psychological' infantilist. I have a deeply ingrained need to be 'babied.' I've been acutely aware of this need or desire since before I started kindergarten. For a time before the advent of the internet, I thought I was likely the only latent baby in the entire world. The first time someone 'babysat' me, the event was transformative. I honestly felt unburdened, liberated, carefree, loved, and cared for … all at once! I've been an occasional toddler ever since.

However, 'psychosexual' infantilists also abound. The Little One who has asked you for the care and has given you this book may well be a psychosexual infantilist … someone who is sexually aroused by being dressed and treated like a baby or toddler. This isn't a response I share – as my babysitters will attest, I'm usually about as limp as linguini while they're caring for me – but it does seem to drive about half of the adult baby community.

However, as a would-be caregiver, you don't have much to worry about. For most psychosexual infantilists, the last thing they will want to do is wind up their playdate and jump on the babysitter. Typically, the Little One will be so grateful for the care and so intent on repeating the

31

experience that any sort of untoward behavior will be out of the question.

If the Little One you're going to babysit is female, you won't see many outward signs of sexual arousal. With males, on the other hand, arousal is often all too evident. If you've ever babysat a 'real' baby boy, you probably know that erections know no age limits. I know I've had occasional erections while being babysat, even though I find the whole experience about as sexually exciting as discussing what I had for lunch.

If you pay as much attention to an adult baby's erection as you would to a baby's – which is no attention at all, really – everything should be fine. Fortunately, erections fold *up,* allowing for erect Little Ones to be cleaned, diapered, and dressed. If I were you, I would not try to fold an erection *down.* Just visualizing such a thing makes me shudder! I imagine the pain would be extraordinary.

Most of my babysitters have exhibited a mile-wide maternal streak. If you have a strong maternal or paternal side, caring for an adult baby can be a hugely rewarding experience ... especially if you have children who now are grown or a little too old to be 'babied'. To that end, I've had several babysitters tell me they were able to do things with me that they never expected to do again!

If you do have a maternal or paternal side, my best advice is to give it free rein. Even if you and your Little One are a tad embarrassed at first, the range of emotions you'll experience during your babysitting sessions make 'stepping out' of a formal, dignity-focused, restrained caregiver role quite rewarding.

I've had several nurses and nurse's aides as babysitters, and the hardest hurdle for them to overcome is what I call the 'dignity issue.' Of course, babies don't have any sort of 'adult dignity' or any sense of modesty. When I'm regressed, I don't, either. However, there's a deeply ingrained tendency in many professional caregivers to treat any adult as an adult patient. That tendency is something these individuals often find very hard to overcome and moving past that sort of training and conditioning requires practice. After an hour or two, you should find that you are able to stop 'seeing' your Little One as an adult and start 'seeing' them as a two-year-old.

The trick, if there is one, is learning to 'see' the Little One in a different way ... in a childlike way, rather than as an adult. That takes a small amount of time, but when it happens, you'll find that any vague discomfort you may have felt at the outset of your time together just drains away.

If you do have a healthcare background, you will likely have a hard time relating all this to the training you've received, which is often inordinately focused on respecting a patient's dignity. I realize that this mental 'switch' may seem quite complicated at this stage. However, a different attitude toward your Little One can be easily internalized, even before your babysitting session begins.

When I try to provide guidance to a neophyte babysitter with a healthcare background, I always tell her:

*I'm a little boy. You can hold me and cuddle me like a kid.*

*I tend to be a messy eater. I don't play with food ... I wear it.*

*Play games when you're feeding me ... landing an airplane, and so on.*

*I'm not in a hospital gown. I'm in a onesie, pajamas, or a diaper shirt.*

*I typically don't know when I wet, so don't ask me if I need to be changed.*

*I don't wear 'briefs,' I wear diapers, and I'm accustomed to diaper checks.*

*You don't have to lift me or carry me, so you can't drop or break me.*

*If I'm coloring or building something, let me finish before you interrupt.*

*If we're playing a board game, you should probably let me win.*

Throw all the 'dignity stuff' out the window when you're caring for your Little One. You'll be doing them a huge service because you'll actually help them regress even more firmly into the baby or toddler role.

Babysitting an adult has to be one of the safest occupations on the planet. I know of no self-respecting adult baby who would want to explain their infantile attire and various props to the police! Still, there's a reason for meeting face-to-face in a public place ahead of any babysitting session. If something 'feels' wrong about the baby – or the babysitter – then there's probably a good reason. I've never met another adult baby I thought harbored malevolent intent of any sort.

Your Little One will likely insist on absolute discretion. This means you cannot share details of your new job opportunity with your spouse or significant other without breaking the confidence you've promised to keep. While you should certainly ensure that someone else knows where you'll be and when you'll be there, sharing the particulars of this sort of work with your friends or significant other is often a mistake. Because our society increasingly sees sexual intent in any interaction between two adults, even close friends will typically jump to erroneous conclusions. Almost certainly, your partner will lack any knowledge of adult babies and infantilism and may go so far as to forbid the encounter.

Years ago, my wife and I became good friends with a young mother who would have made an ideal babysitter. The lady herself was eager to have the job, and I know the income would have been a blessing to her and her family. Unfortunately, she broke our confidence and told her husband about the sort of work she'd be doing. In response, her husband put his foot down. We still saw the couple socially, but our interactions with them were strained, to say the least.

Many Little Ones make full disclosure of their infantilism to their spouses or Significant Others, but quite a few manage to keep their secret hidden ... sometimes, for years and years. The reason for the lack of open dialogue on the subject is that many spouses or Significant Others – usually women – evidence strong negative reactions to their partner wearing diapers and baby clothes. I've been very lucky because my Significant Other actively participates in my care and still enjoys babying me. Schedules being what they are, however, I have outside babysitters in from time to time.

If you're female and you've been asked to care for a male, you may feel vaguely uneasy. Do you have an open-minded, non-judgmental, and discrete girlfriend who can accompany you to the first babysitting session? She doesn't have to participate, or even watch, but she can be on hand to ensure that nothing untoward happens. Over the years, I've had several new babysitters bring friends with them. In one instance, my new babysitter couldn't make the job fit her busy nursing schedule, but her friend – also a young nurse – wound up babysitting me almost every week for more than a year.

Let's assume that you'd like to try babysitting a Little One. You can do several things to more effectively 'set the stage' for your first babysitting session. Decide whether you want your Little One to be 'all dressed' and waiting for you when you arrive, or whether they'll come to you wearing street clothes over a diaper. I've found that having a new babysitter undress and then 'dress' me is awkward. In my view, it is much easier for any caregiver to just 'dive in' to caring for a small child rather than help me make the transition from the adult world to infancy.

For that reason, I'm almost always wearing baby clothes and sitting on the floor playing with my toy trains or Tinkertoys when a babysitter arrives. Most of the time, she will sit down and begin playing with me. That's quite a nice way to break the ice. Many regressed adults tend to 'zone out' and become low verbal. For me, the outside world seems to melt away. For whatever reason, that's a harder state to achieve when I must undress, pick out baby clothes, and let someone else dress me.

My pet peeve when I'm being babysat is decision-making. I know toddlers love to be given options from which to choose. In my case, however, having to make a decision or make a choice is a sure way to bring the adult world crashing back in. Perhaps the most effective way of setting the stage for a babysitting session is to have a care plan. This doesn't have to be an elaborate written schedule, but a few notes on an index card will go a long way to helping you take action steps without requiring input from your Little One.

If you have some actual babysitting or healthcare experience, developing a care plan will probably be quite easy. If you lack experience caring for someone else, a care plan can be a daunting task. For a typical four-hour babysitting session, a rudimentary care plan might look like this:

*Playtime*

*Bottle and burp*

*Diaper change*

*A board game*

*Television or DVD*

*Diaper change*

*Feed baby food*

*Coloring with Crayons*

*Exercise*

*Bathtime*

*Diaper and dress*

*Nap*

*Bottle and burp*

*Diaper change*

*Television or DVD*

You'll notice that certain activities tend to be repeated. In four hours' time, for example, you can easily feed two bottles, change three diapers, and so on. A good babysitting session is built on this sort of repetition since it provides your Little One with a routine they can depend upon in future sessions.

Over time, you can discard activities that you or your Little One don't enjoy and substitute new activities in their place. Preparation is the key, along with thinking ahead about your time together, frank dialogue about what you enjoy and don't enjoy, and sharing ideas for improvement.

I've seen 'real' babies wearing bibs embroidered with "Spit happens." Other things happen too, and despite your best planning or intentions, you cannot adequately prepare for them. Years ago, for example, my wife interrupted an out-of-town babysitting session to tell me that my mother had passed away quite suddenly. I literally had to pick myself up off the floor and prepare for a long trip to be with my family. Of course, there's no way any babysitting session can recover from that sort of blow.

But smaller things can also conspire to rob you and your Little One of carefully planned time together. I've had family emergencies derail a babysitting session in progress, had some minor health issues flare at that moment, and even been so sleep-deprived that I just slept the entire time away. A babysitter once overslept, incredibly enough, and missed our time altogether. As I say, things happen. How you deal with them – and how you let them affect you and your babysitting routine – will depend in large measure on how well-prepared you are for spending time with your Little One.

Don't prejudge *your* ability to experience happiness and fulfillment while caring for a Little One. If you allow yourself the opportunity to enjoy providing the care, you may find that you experience the same sort of fulfillment and exhilaration most of us Little Ones feel when we're receiving unbridled attention. While you may not feel indescribable joy right away, increased familiarity with the baby care routine may eventually help you 'squeeze the trigger' on positive, productive, and enjoyable emotions. At the very least, such familiarity will allow you to share the sense of soothing calm you provide your Little One.

In all my years, I've had only one babysitter seize the opportunity to care for me because she was enamored of me. I'm certainly not unlovable, but I've been in a serious relationship most of my adult life and this woman knew I was not looking for any sort of romantic involvement. My 'big baby' relationship with this lady began with a brief mechanical session, which went well enough. When she came back to babysit, I gradually became aware that she was far more excited than was perhaps normal. The fault was mine since I had not imagined I'd have someone lusting after me while changing my diaper!

On the other hand: Years ago, when I was approaching middle age, I 'fell' for a babysitter. The attraction was *not* mutual, and the young woman wasn't even particularly maternal. Just be forewarned: Emotional involvement can happen quickly between a big baby and their caregiver. If that's something you both want, great! If not, you'll need to be aware of your respective situations and savvy enough to avoid any romantic pitfalls.

If all this paints a different picture of adult babies than you've gotten from the internet or cable TV, great! If you're beginning to rethink some of your initial conceptions of infantilism and caring for a Little One, then I've achieved my goal. I can tell you from vast personal experience: Babysitting a Little One is a peaceful, calming, benign interaction. Almost every babysitter I've had absolutely loved the experience. Most told me how much they adored our time together, and most could not wait for a chance to come back.

Among my score of babysitters, I've had:

- Nursing students and nurse's aides
- A pediatric Registered Nurse
- Several schoolteachers
- Three stay-at-home moms

• Two professional nannies

• A retired Carmelite nun

Every single individual was a stranger to adult babies when she came to care for me. Each one will tell you that I treated them like princesses ... to me, they are all Pearls of Great Price. I was never anything less than completely respectful of their time. I went out of my way to demonstrate to them how appreciative I was for the care. My babysitters have, almost without exception, become good friends and I continue to cherish those relationships even after they've gone on to other jobs or other places.

In the final analysis, perhaps the biggest hurdle you must cross is the notion that someone who *wants* care must also *need* it. I'm a perfectly healthy adult, but my need is *mental* ... something no one can see. I need to return periodically to a time when I had no worries, no decisions to make, and someone there to care for me. The fact that I wear baby clothes, eat in a highchair, and nap in a crib is probably incidental to the discussion.

I'm unsure why such a stigma still surrounds anyone above the age of 3 who still wants to be a baby. I genuinely wish that weren't the case, but it is. The wide availability of 'incontinence' products – with many popular brands and styles clearly created especially for the adult baby community – tells us that adults in diapers are an increasingly significant component of modern society.

The ranks of Little Ones are obviously expanding at an exponential rate, and I can find no credible or rational explanation for the associated hysteria. Why we should be alarmed or frightened of these folks? As Rosalie Bent noted earlier in this book, anyone who is 'different' is a target for marginalization. I cannot understand how being 'different' makes us a threat, but that's the way of the world.

Pop writers and bloggers don't have to work very hard to make infantilists sound like 'different' people, but the fact remains that we are just like everyone else. We need the same love and attention that everyone needs, but we choose to receive it at a childlike level.

You will be doing your Little One – and yourself – a big favor if you choose to step out in faith and offer your time and experience to someone who wants desperately to experience being a baby or toddler again. Infantilism, regardless of the root causes, is typically *progressive.* That means that if you like the job, and the Little One benefits from the care you've provided, you can continue to babysit for a long time.

In a dangerous and uncertain world, caring for a Little One is like a warm blanket ... it serves to remind you, if only for a few hours here and there, that there's a genuine bond that connects you to another human being. That connection is a rare and special thing these days.

# 4. | Dress, Rehearsal

**M**any years ago, a mentor I respected gave me what I considered sage advice: *Be quick to make up your mind, and slow to change it.* As I've grown older, however, the wisdom of that guidance has been sorely tested.

Some of the greatest experiences I've had would not have been possible had I rejected them out-of-hand, as I am wont to do. I've knelt in the grotto where Jesus was born, had an infant African gorilla brush past my leg while on a safari, and lived in great cities like London, Los Angeles, and New York. None of those things would have happened had I not spent time thinking about them rather than deciding immediately against them.

With that thought in mind, this is an opportune time for a little litmus test. As you're giving thought to being a possible part-time caregiver to an adult baby, what is your mind? Are you thinking the whole enterprise sounds like fun? Are you thinking it's not for you? Are you still wondering if you can do this and if everything will work out?

I ask because this little chapter is a turning point of sorts. The remainder of this book is largely instructional in nature. If you're already firmly of the opinion that big babysitting isn't something you want to try, you might just as well stop reading. If you're on the fence, I'd ask you to finish this chapter and the next, then ask yourself how you feel. If you think you're ready to get started, this chapter and those that follow will help you visualize important techniques. Perhaps most importantly, you'll be able to 'see' yourself caring for a Little One.

Before you book a babysitting session, you'll need a good understanding of the clothing available to adult babies these days. Clothing for a baby boy differs from clothing for a baby girl, of course, and there are some subtle distinctions when compared to actual infant clothing.

To start, let's talk about clothing that is adaptable to – and worn by – both male and female infantilists. Although the term 'onesie' means different things in different parts of the world, it has a singularly simple meaning for big babies:

A onesie is a bodysuit that has a snap closure at the crotch and does not cover the legs.

Adult baby onesies come in a variety of fabrics and are sold by more than a dozen different suppliers.  Some have babyish icons or imagery embroidered on the front, across the chest, while others are plain white. One of my white onesies is a shortall since my legs are covered to just above the knee. Typically, onesies have short sleeves, like a t-shirt.

The principal advantages of a onesie include the ease of putting it on an adult – most onesies have necks that are very stretchy – and the row of snaps at the bottom, which make for easy dressing and changing. Typically, the snaps are metal, since plastic snaps don't stay closed and lack the authenticity many infantilists demand. The type of snap used is a telltale sign: If the onesie snaps with plastic snaps, it was probably made by a work-at-home mom. Plastic snaps are typically cheaper. Metal snaps, on the other hand, require a snap press and are the hallmark of a professional tailor or larger manufacturer.

When I was a young adult years ago, onesies in adult sizes simply did not exist. I had a talented seamstress who custom-made baby clothes for me. Today, there's quite a choice … and quite a demand.

Adult diaper shirts are a staple in my baby wardrobe. Many of my diaper shirts have embroidery on the front, and most stop just short of my waist. Since I live in a hot climate, I wear diaper shirts almost year-round. If your Little One has no big baby clothing, a nice diaper shirt would be a good first investment. These are not inexpensive, but quality diaper shirts will last and last.

Snap-shoulder shirts are still quite popular. The typical baby snap shirt, scaled up, doesn't work well with adults because of the expanse of the chest, but shirts with snap shoulders are a nice touch. These are

43

pulled over the head, then the shoulder snaps up with two or three snaps. Some snap-shoulder shirts have a pacifier loop on the other shoulder, through which you can loop a lanyard or pacifier keeper. My seamstress adds a pacifier loop to almost everything she makes for me.

The real difference between onesies, diaper shirts, and snap-shoulder shirts for big boys and girls is largely in the color of the fabric and, occasionally, the trim.

Adult baby pajamas come in several styles. You may remember the all-in-one Dr. Denton footed pajamas available when you were a child. Scaled-up versions are available to infantilists today. However, they are bulky, hard to get into and out of, and rather warm. Other pajamas are available without the feet, and still others are two-piece. Quite often, the two-piece variety has 'shorty' pants.

Many adult babies long for a big sleeper, then discover how difficult they are to put on and remove. I haven't found that the process is any easier when there's a babysitter involved. For me, sleeper-style pajamas are just too much trouble, and I vastly prefer two-piece pajamas instead.

Both boy and girl big babies wear adult bonnets that typically tie beneath the chin. Also available are adult baby caps that look a good deal like the little caps hospitals put on newborns. Typically, these come in pastel colors and lively prints.

Adult baby mittens are also available. Like bonnets and caps, mittens don't seem to be used exclusively by one gender. I have one set of mittens, and they are especially useful when I try to regress since they make any sort of 'adulting' rather difficult. If you find yourself caring for a 'grabby' baby, mittens may help you solve the problem of keeping little hands where they should be.

I asked an adult baby girl I know to tell me about the baby clothing in her closet since I'm not an authority. She says the categories are best broken down as onesies, which we've already discussed, as well as sets, dresses, and individual items.

44

This young lady says her onesies tend to be her favorite color or a pastel color or print. Most of them have some kind of frill, ruffle, or collar. She does note, however, that a plain onesie – with no frills – is an essential element of her wardrobe as well.

She also has a pair of footie pajamas, just as I did years ago. One of her favorite items has a onesie bottom and an overall-like top, which allows her to wear a t-shirt or diaper shirt underneath.

"Sets," she explained to me, "are just a top and a bottom that go together. I have a set that is like a short dress with some bloomers, and two that are shirts and shorts in cute babyish prints. I have a matching bib and bloomers as well."

Adult baby dresses are comfortable and adorable. As my friend notes, "My dresses are a lot more girly with frills and lace. I have two dedicated 'little' dresses. However, I have plenty of other dresses that aren't necessarily 'little' but will pass for it. A lot of the clothes I wear on a normal day would work well as little clothes. I think women have a lot more leeway in terms of dressing 'little' and recent fashion trends – like pleated skirts and skirt-alls – help with that."

My friend doesn't overstate the ease with which seemingly innocuous women can slip into the big baby role. Women can wear 'baby fresh' scents, lounge with stuffed toys, and wear babyish clothing with little fear of ridicule. Had I tried to do the same thing when I was this young lady's age, I'd probably have been beaten up and left for dead. Fortunately, times change.

Compared to the clothing available for big baby girls, clothing for big baby boys is straightforward. For example, I have two shortalls. One is actually a bib overall with short legs and snaps in the crotch, and it makes me look like a toddler train engineer. Since I love playing with toy trains when I regress, this is as it should be. Overalls are also available – sometimes with snaps all the way up and down the inside legs – as are cargo shorts with snaps and so on.

Gender is the top identifying factor for a child and for a Little One as well. Gender is obvious very early on in an infant's life. Gender is normally connected to physiology, but in the case of a Little One, gender can be a fluid thing. A penis doesn't necessarily mean your Little One is male! Around half of physically male Little Ones identify as female, or 'sissy'.

Many 'sissy' Little Ones regress as a stylized, over-the-top expression of femininity that isn't quite accurate. At best, they are portraying the 'image' of the female, and you'll see rows and rows of lace and frills along with excessively infantile or feminine clothing.

Your Little's wardrobe will tell you a great deal about them … including their gender. An adult baby male who dresses as a girl is cross-dressing in the classic sense, but cross-dressing isn't true gender confusion. Instead, wearing little girl clothes is little more than role-playing or enjoying the crossing of gender boundaries.

An adult male will often be happily male and heterosexual, yet the same male, as the Little One you care for, may be a female or sissy. This gender confusion is normally just in males, but it is not unknown in females. You'll need to keep an open mind until you are sure.

Now, far more than in years past, children's clothes and toys can be gender neutral. Typically, Little Ones will select obvious gender-specific clothes, as if to loudly proclaim who they are. This tendency crosses over into toys as well, which might explain why your male Little One has a few baby dolls about.

A few Little Ones don't really show a gender preference and apparently don't really care.

This gender-related information will be useful if you plan a 'mechanical session' as an introduction to your Little One and big babysitting. I'd highly recommend that you plan a 'mechanical session' if you don't know your Little One all that well or if you have never seen their big baby 'stash' of clothing and supplies. If your Little One is 'hiding' a sissy or girly adult baby wardrobe, you'll have a chance to see it firsthand. You'll then be able to alter your interactions to reflect the gender of choice.

At the start of one of these purely mechanical sessions, you should ask your Little One to show you all their baby things. This might be nearly nothing at all, there might be quite an ensemble, or there might be an entire nursery. What you see will help you settle the gender issue with some immediacy.

At the outset, look for three things: A diaper, a pacifier, and a baby bottle. Pick up the diaper and pacifier and carry them with you. If you're not already there, have your Little One take you to the room they want to use as a nursery, which can run the gamut from a fully furnished 'baby room' to a typical bedroom and everything in between.

Help your Little One undress or ask them to undress in front of you. They can hand you their clothes and you can fold them neatly. Whatever they're wearing, they will not be needing it for the next couple of hours. For the Little One, a brief 'mechanical session' has one key benefit: The adult baby becomes accustomed to being naked in front of you. Don't rob your big baby of that benefit.

This is a more important benefit than you might think. Many Little Ones are effectively sticking their toe into the water the first time a prospective caregiver sees them naked or in baby clothes. This is because they're unsure how you will react. You may be unsure, too!

If you know even a few minutes ahead of time what to expect, you can handle your baby's embarrassment without so much as a broad smile. You're in charge, and you should act like it. Be straightforward and to the point.

Once you've gotten your big baby undressed, sit and have your Little One stand in front of you. Ask them about any ongoing medical issues and have them explain their answers. Don't be afraid to touch their body, and don't be in a hurry to get them dressed. This is valuable information-gathering time for you, and what the Little One tells you now will shape and mold your first few babysitting sessions. At this point, there's no need to baby-talk. Interact with your big baby as you would with an adult.

While you have the opportunity, check for an overage of pubic hair. Many adult baby girls are clean-shaven, but adult baby boys often sport a jungle of 'down-there' hair. This is important because having to clean up pubic hair inordinately complicates diaper changes. If you have a healthcare background, you may feel competent enough to suggest that you help your Little One trim 'down there.' If not, perhaps you could tactfully suggest that your big baby trim the hair themselves.

A word of caution: Don't be quick to grab scissors or a razor unless you're sure you know what you are doing. Years ago, a babysitter who was trying to be helpful managed to nick a hair follicle on my thigh with a razor, and the resulting infection required surgery before it finally healed.

My very first babysitter introduced me to what she called the 'Magic Bracelet.' This was simply a thin strip of elastic-backed cloth, sewn together, which I wore on my wrist while she babysat me. Our agreement was that any time I had the 'Magic Bracelet' in place, I had to be her baby or toddler … I could not behave as if I were more than about three years old. Her stipulations were more detailed, but you get the idea.

Anyway, the 'Magic Bracelet' had a transformative effect on my babysitting interactions with my first few babysitters. You can use a hair scrunchy for a 'Magic Bracelet' if you like. The first 'Magic Bracelet' I had predated hair scrunchies by more than a decade. If you like the idea, make up a 'Magic Bracelet' ahead of your mechanical session and take it with you. Once you've completed your assessment of your big baby, put the 'Magic Bracelet' on them and explain the concept.

Following your initial 'examination,' you might consider a quick bath time. A word of caution here: If you're not certain your big baby can get *out* of a bathtub, don't get them into it! So many home-related accidents happen in the bathroom that it just makes sense to be extraordinarily cautious. I'll belabor this point in an entire chapter on bathing, but you should keep it in mind.

If you're not physically able to help your Little One out of a bathtub, or if you're not sure your big baby can get out on their own, then you'll need to come up with a creative option. Voloh's bath illustration (Chapter 8) is a bit fanciful, but in some situations, a bathtub that isn't a bathtub is required. Portable bathtubs are typically not inexpensive, but they are certainly worthwhile in certain situations.

You don't really need bubble bath or toys for this first quick bath. Just fill the bathtub, get your Little One into it, and sit beside the tub and use a washcloth to give them a babyish bath. Put a pacifier in their mouth and tell them you expect them to be a two-year-old for the rest of your time together.

The whole bath interlude might take 10 minutes. Again, use care as the baby steps out of the tub. My babysitters always help me stand and often have their arm around my torso to ensure I do not fall.

Dry off your Little One and make sure they aren't cold. Take them back to their bedroom or nursery and have them lie face-down on the bed or whatever, then give a baby massage. Use Baby Magic or a similar lotion if they have it. The massage helps you overcome any shyness about touching your Little One's body, and – for the big baby – your touch is a wonderful thing. Your kiddo might well be close to falling asleep when you finish.

Have your big baby turn over so you can diaper them. I'll discuss diapering techniques in another chapter but suffice it to say this may be the first time since they were potty trained that anyone has put a diaper on them. Don't worry about baby lotion or powder. Instead, take your time and focus on the fit of the diaper. Have your Little One sit up so you can slip on a t-shirt, onesie, or babyish top of some type. With the pacifier still in, your adult baby won't be able to comment. You will, however, be able to tell if they're uncomfortable for some reason.

Next, find the baby bottle you located at the beginning of your visit. Open their refrigerator and fill the bottle with about eight ounces of whatever you can find … juice or milk would be ideal. Also locate a kitchen towel of some sort, which will serve as a burp cloth. I always keep a stack of baby diapers on my highchair tray because I tend to go through quite a few burp clothes in a babysitting session. However, few big babies are as well-prepared as I am!

Take the bottle with you. Ideally, you'll find an uncluttered place on the carpet to sit. Have your big baby sit down beside you. You can either have the Little One lie down and sit by them, feeding the bottle, or they can lie with their head in your lap. Either works fine, but having your big baby lie in the lap may feel like an intimate act. If you're not ready for that just yet, then you can just sit beside them.

Hold the bottle while your Little One is nursing. When they've finished, have them sit up, face you, and then burp them. There's specific information on burping later in this book.

Once you've fed the bottle and burped the baby, use the rest of your time together for a heart-to-heart talk. Stay seated on the floor and ask:

• What do you really want from our time together?

• Do you think you'll want me to babysit on a regular basis?

• To what do you look forward with the greatest anticipation?

• Can you be all dressed and ready to play when I arrive?

These four questions go to the heart of your Little One's desire for a caregiver. The final couple of questions also effectively set the stage for your first real babysitting session ... and perhaps, for babysitting sessions that follow. Once you've listened to your big baby – really *listened* – then you can share any constraints, stipulations, or concerns you have. Be sure to let your Little One speak first, and to their hearts' content. Only when people feel you've really listened to them are they usually inclined to give you their undivided attention. In this case, you want to make sure your Little One understands and can appreciate any reservations you have.

Wrap up your little 'mechanical session' by doing a quick diaper check. You can gently squeeze the front of the diaper or, if you're feeling adventurous, slip a finger inside the waistband or leg gathers. Since your big baby likely hasn't regressed during your time together, the diaper may not be wet at all. If the diaper *is* wet, however, you'll have an opportunity to develop your diaper-changing skills. I'll talk more about diapers and changing routines in a forthcoming chapter.

Take your Little One by the hand, tell them what you're going to do next, then lead them back to their changing space. This will likely be the same spot where you diapered them at the beginning of your time together.

# 5. | Nap and Playtime

I was a big M*A*S*H fan back in the day, and I avidly watch the episodes even today. In one 1975 installment, Colonel Potter read from a Garand rifle field manual to put some traumatized Korean kids to sleep. Obviously, Colonel Potter couldn't speak Korean, and the kids didn't understand English.

The children were all asleep after about three paragraphs. Colonel Potter tucked them in and said, "And so, they lived happily ever after." May that be true for all of us!

What Harry Morgan's stellar performance taught me is that intonation and animation play a far bigger role in bedtime stories than content. When a babysitter reads a Dr. Seuss or Thomas the Tank Engine book to put me to sleep, I stop paying attention to grammar and pronunciation – a rare thing for a writer! – and focus instead on the tone and cadence of her voice.

I count on my 'little time' to be a genuinely restful experience. I guess that's why I place such importance on naps. For me, being put down for a nap is often the pinnacle of a babysitting interlude. One of my babysitters was a retired Carmelite nun who had overseen an orphanage for 20 years. Having her put me to bed was a sublime experience ... one I miss very much.

Melissa always made sure I was physically tired and ready for a nap. This usually isn't particularly difficult since I have chronic insomnia. Twenty years ago, however, some bit of exercise would often do the trick. Melissa would take me out in our fenced backyard and have me chase after a tennis ball or something. In the hot summertime, she pulled out my old Slip 'N Slide. Wearing a diaper and plastic pants on a Slip 'N Slide adds an element of danger that I wouldn't recommend, but I managed to emerge unscathed. Over time, I found that sort of physical exertion helpful because it made me nearly ready to settle down and sleep for a few minutes.

Once back inside, Melissa usually hustled me into the bathtub. I'll write in detail about bath times later in this book, but I found that being bathed was an even better prelude to being able to fall asleep and sleep for a quarter-hour or so. I would often step from the bathtub, stand on the mat while Melissa dried me, and then head straight for the bed or changing table so she could dress me for sleep.

Most times, I nap wearing nothing more than a diaper shirt and a diaper. In those days, I would climb into my crib and lie down on the ancient mattress. Melissa would cover me with the thin crib blanket I still use, and then she'd sit on the edge of the 'big' bed and read to me. I usually closed my eyes within 30 seconds and was asleep in a minute or less. Melissa would put the book down and stand beside my crib, stroking my hair for a few minutes, while she made sure I was asleep. How I wish some of the babysitters I've had since could master Melissa's technique!

If your Little One doesn't have a crib, you can put them down for a nap wherever they're accustomed to sleeping. I've even curled up and gone to sleep in a baby's playpen! A bed is just fine. In a pinch, even the floor will work. Creature comforts are important, however. Make sure there's something covering the big baby, but don't pile on too many blankets. Diapers and baby clothes tend to be hotter than typical adult sleep attire.

If there's a television on somewhere in the house or apartment, turn it off. If there's a lamp or light nearby, be sure to turn it out. If you find that you need a light to read a bedtime story, try downloading the book on your cellphone and using the cellphone instead. You'll want to pay close attention to your Little One as you read. Even if you're not possessed of Colonel Potter's sort of reading skill, you usually won't need to read much!

The length of the nap I can take varies according to my general fatigue and how 'active' my insomnia is, but I can usually sleep for 15 minutes or more. A few times, I've slept for an hour or longer, but that's rare. You can reliably expect your Little One to be sleeping for a quarter-hour or so if you put them to bed correctly, so nap routines are an important babysitting skill to master. Once your big baby is sleeping, you have a little free time to check your cell phone, tidy up the house or just enjoy some well-deserved peace and quiet.

As often as not, Melissa would be sitting on the 'big' bed, waiting for me to wake up. On those occasions when she wasn't there and I was alone, I would sometimes begin to cry. I seldom had to cry more than a couple of minutes before she was back in the room. Crying is an important skill for Little Ones to relearn, and crying was a struggle for me

55

at first. These days, it's second nature. As a babysitter, however, you'll have to adapt to the sight and sound of a chronological adult crying. Seeing and hearing an adult cry for the first time can be upsetting, to say the least. For some adult babies, crying comes quite naturally. I've had to actively relearn how to cry!

A post-nap routine is, in many ways, just as important as how you put your Little One down. If I was awake and crying, Melissa would walk to the side of the crib and hug me for a few minutes, letting me cry into her shoulder. Other babysitters have had me lie back down while I continued to cry, content to pat my back or stroke my hair until I've finished. Some years ago, I had a pediatric nurse practitioner babysit me several times, and she always brought a baby wipe to the crib with her. She'd wipe my face and my hands, which I found quite refreshing. She'd also check my temperature, for whatever reason, which I came to find quite reassuring.

Once you have your Little One back up with their feet on the floor, take a moment to check for the usual baby comforts. For example:

- Is the diaper wet?
- If so, were there any leaks?
- What sort of clothing should I put on next?

The reason for the 'leak check' is purely personal: I don't like to climb back into my crib a few days later and find that the crib sheet and mattress had gotten wet during the last babysitting interlude! Some big babies are heavy wetters, especially while they're down for a nap. If you discover that a diaper has done a less-than-stellar job of handling what your Little One dished out, at least let them know that some cleanup may be necessary after you've gone.

Almost without exception, I am very wet when I wake from a nap, so I must lie down for a diaper change, and then I'm dressed in something more substantial. Unless it's hot summertime, you probably won't want your big baby to spend the rest of your time together wearing just a diaper shirt. Depending on the skill of the babysitter, this post-nap changing and dressing routine can take nearly as much time as the nap itself.

Keep in mind that most Little Ones regress to the point that waking from a nap is quite an ordeal. Recall the sort of fog that envelopes you after a good night's sleep, then multiply that a time or two. That's the sort of pervasive 'out of it' feeling an adult baby typically experiences when they wake from a nap. You'll need to give them a few minutes to get back to speed. Some of my babysitters have made allowances for this, letting me lie on my changing pad for a few minutes while they dressed me or gently massaged my hands or feet.

Once your Little One is fully awake, you'll typically find that they are at least a little hungry. A bottle or a snack should be next on your agenda. I'll address feeding dynamics later in this book.

Playtime is typically the opposite of putting an adult baby down for a nap because play should enliven or excite your Little One. If this is the first babysitting experience for your big baby, they may not have much in the way of toys. Whatever your Little One has will likely be enough, and you can add to the collection over time. Over the years, I have learned that a toy box is a useful thing. Mine is now almost completely full.

Some babysitters – usually middle-aged and older – find that they enjoy the play interludes even more than the Little One. I guess that's to be expected, but I still find it a little disconcerting. I've had several babysitters spend a half-hour playing with my Play-Doh Fun Factory! Others have brought along well-loved board games and taught me to play. As it happens, my play level is slightly advanced for my 'little' age. So long as the game doesn't require your Little One to be particularly verbal, you should give it a try. Admittedly, this tends to rule out several of the 'audience participation' party games that are popular nowadays.

As a 'real' kid, I was fascinated by trains. Today, I have a huge train table and I enjoy moving the wooden trains around the tracks and rearranging the buildings, cars, and people. When a babysitter walks through my front door, that's what she typically finds me doing ... playing with trains.

For a play interlude, however, I prefer something more interactive. This doesn't mean that you *must* get on the floor and play with me, but it helps! However, playtime is, by nature, very individual. For example, many Little Ones enjoy coloring. I find it tedious and uncomfortable. You'll need a little trial and error to determine what your big baby enjoys.

If you need some playtime ideas beyond Crayons and Play-Doh, here's a list to start:

**A floor puzzle** can be quite challenging for 15 minutes or so. Look for a 100-piece puzzle or something a little smaller. I still have an old Batman puzzle I bought years and years ago and still enjoy putting it together. Puzzles on the dining table have a way of needing a couple of babysitting sessions to complete, while floor puzzles can usually be finished in a few minutes.

**Wooden blocks** are a time-tested favorite. Several modern permutations include Lincoln Logs and the astonishingly expensive Kapla blocks. I've found that I quite enjoy construction sets of various types. When I was a grade-schooler, I had one of the big Kenner Girder and Panel sets. I still have it, tucked away beneath my bed, and play with it quite often when I'm being babysat.

**Playmobil sets, Legos, Duplo,** and others are wonderful for diverse play. Some of the modern Lego sets, although quite expensive, can provide enough building fun to last over several babysitting sessions. K'Nex sets are also a good option, although most – like my roller coaster – are designed for slightly older kids than I like to be. Frankly, the K'Nex Budding Builders set is more my speed.

**Diecast cars and trucks** are just as much fun now as they were when you were little. Adult babies make for more energetic play than toddlers do, so you may need a little bigger area. That living room that easily accommodated a couple of three-year-old boys playing with Tonka trucks may now be too small. Hot Wheels tracks tend to be more compact these days than the living room layouts we had when I was little. Perhaps as impressive, Hot Wheels can still be bought for a dollar, making them easy acquisitions. I can still make a play session out of running my just-purchased Hot Wheels down the hallway.

**Simple board or card games** can be a significant challenge, especially if you haven't played them in many years. One of my caregivers has a huge affinity for checkers and loves to tell me she's won. I quite enjoy Chutes and Ladders and Candy Land. My first babysitter loved to play The Game of Life, even though it was a little too advanced for a little kid like me. Years ago, I had a babysitter fling a deck of cards into the air and scream, "52 card pickup!" Whatever works, I suppose.

**Dolls** are still a favorite among female ABs ... and some males as well. While I don't have that 'little girl' side, I understand that the American Girl series of dolls make quite good playthings for adult babies.

**A sketchbook** allows me to draw, and I'll happily draw for a half-hour or so at a time. As a writer, I keyboard all day, and my wrists and fingers aren't accustomed to being pressed into use, so the amount of time I can spend drawing is constrained. Drawing was encouraged when I was growing up, and both my brother and I went through reams of paper. While I don't like to color – the texture of typical coloring book paper is just too rough for me – I am glad I have re-discovered the joys of drawing as an infantilist. Colored pencils, felt-tip pens, and even ball-point pens are excellent modern-day replacements for the thick markers that were available when I was a 'real' kid. Some years ago, I bought a spiral-bound sketchbook so I could keep all my creations in one place. I do admit to having an Etch-A-Sketch – another garage sale find – but as a creative outlet, I find it frustrating. Several of my babysitters have loved playing with it. If your Little One doesn't enjoy coloring or cannot be constrained to stay within the lines, try a sketchbook instead.

**Watercolors** can be messy but are lots of fun. Just have some paper towels on hand to wipe up the inevitable spill. While some big babies enjoy finger painting, I've found it fun only for a very brief time.

After that, the challenge becomes cleanup, which often takes longer than the finger-painting interlude itself.

**Craft kits** abound, using all sorts of media and textures we hadn't even thought of when I was growing up. At Christmas time, craft ornaments are particularly appropriate. One of my favorite babysitters showed up for each babysitting session with a new craft kit, purloined from Walmart or Target. She seemed to have a new craft each time she came to care for me. I loved seeing what she would bring us!

None of this needs to cost very much. As Melissa used to remind me, garage sales were invented to provide affordable playthings for infantilists. She was a terrific garage- and yard sale shopper, and she had the ability to recall what I already had and did not have. Perhaps more to the point, all those years caring for kids in the convent taught her which toys still had life left in them and which she should pass by.

Although I enjoy watching DVDs and kid's programs on television, I don't really think of anything television based as a play activity. As an adult, I've developed a healthy appreciation for the kind of saint that Fred Rogers obviously was, and I still enjoy watching Thomas the Tank Engine DVDs. I also have all three of the Cars movies and enjoy watching a segment of first one and then another. I admit to having to exert some effort to keep up with the plots, but that's hardly the fault of the animators at Pixar.

However, I do know some adult babies who have vintage PlayStations® and the like and enjoy playing simple games while they're being babysat. Years ago, a babysitter brought her Wii, and we played a variety of two-person games, like Mario Kart. Even a game on a tablet or your cellphone will make for an interesting interlude. If you're inclined toward gaming, video games that allow you to involve both yourself and your big baby are the way to go.

If your playtime extends more than, say, a half-hour, you might be wise to ask your Little One to stand up so you can do a quick diaper check. As I've mentioned, a diaper check for an adult baby is very similar to a diaper check for a 'real' baby and needn't be particularly elaborate. Usually, just a look will often tell you if the diaper is only moderately wet or close to being overloaded. If you decide that your big baby needs to be changed right away, there's no need to interrupt what they're doing. Instead, find something to use as a changing pad and have them lie on the floor, surrounded by their toys. Once you finish, they can go right back to playing.

Playtime can be as loud or as quiet as you like. You must set the tone! Don't expect your big baby to jump and shout without some encouragement. Keep the dialogue going and don't let your Little One get too immersed in whatever activity you've provided.

Finally, don't forget how much of a play motivator *time* can be. Set a finite period for play and stick to it. There's nothing wrong with telling a big baby that they have 30 minutes to play. When you've run through the allotted minutes, tell your big baby that they have exactly two minutes (or three, or four) to clean everything up. Then, watch them pick everything up! Inevitably, they'll miss something, and you can seize the opportunity to lead your Little One by the hand to complete the task you've assigned. Nothing will make them feel more like a child, and that's the goal.

# 6. | Bottles, Burping and Baby Food

or many adult babysitters, ensuring that their Little One is properly hydrated and nourished is the most enjoyable part of the caregiving interlude. I've had so many babysitters fall asleep while feeding me a bottle that I've come to expect it.

Baby bottles have come a long way from the plastic, latex-nipple nursers my mother used when I was a baby. Nowadays, nipples are expected to look something like a mother's anatomy. In my day, that was never the case. Today's nipples tend to be 'slower,' but as far as most adult babies are concerned, that's a minor detriment.

I still have a couple of plastic bottles purchased early on in my renewed childhood, and I vastly prefer the modern variety. Many are ergonomically designed to be easier for little hands to hold, and most won't break or shatter if they are accidentally dropped.

Your Little One will likely have at least a couple of baby bottles on hand. If you can't find them during your brief 'mechanical' session, be sure they're bought, washed, and ready for your first babysitting interlude. Stores like Target and Walmart have a wide variety of bottles on the shelves. My current favorites are Avent, made by Phillips Corporation. I like the shape of the bottles, and the nipples are easy for an adult mouth to work. The Nuk Simply Natural bottles and nipples are a good choice as well.

As cute as the small four-ounce baby bottles are, they're not practical for an adult baby. Small bottles are drained far too quickly. You'll need something with at least an eight-ounce capacity. The Avent bottles hold that much liquid easily. I have also tried several of the 'adult' baby bottles on the market. They're made of glass, and they're really heavy. I don't find the larger nipple particularly helpful.

Just as important as the baby bottle is the liquid that fills it. If your Little One isn't lactose intolerant, milk is always a good choice. I am lactose intolerant, so I drink vanilla-flavored Silk, which is a high-end soymilk product. I also enjoy apple juice and, on occasion, Gatorade. I find most other juices cloying and the other sports drinks on the market are a little too sugary for my taste.

Ideally, your big baby should have a couple of bottles made up and waiting for you in the refrigerator. I always make sure to have three bottles waiting before any babysitting session. You may need to give rather pointed instructions on this point or be prepared to arrive with a well-stocked diaper bag. Again, the brief 'mechanical' session should show you what your Little One has and lacks.

Unlike most other babysitting activities, you can feed a bottle almost anywhere. The reason I recommend sitting on the floor during your 'mechanical' session is that it is usually very easy for a neophyte caregiver to manage a big baby on the floor. Unlike 'real' baby care, you don't *have* to feed a bottle to a big baby with the baby in your lap. However, you'll probably find that your lap is the most natural – and realistic – place to feed a bottle.

I'd recommend that you create a cellphone playlist of some nursery songs or music and have that playlist playing quietly while you feed your Little One. For that matter, the same soundtrack can accompany you from bottle feeding to diaper changing, bathing, and almost everything else you do. The kiddy music is a very nice touch. I like it because it has a calming effect on me and keeps my babysitter focused on treating me as a toddler.

The natural progression of a babysitting session will likely have you deciding to sit on the sofa and feed your big baby there. Once you do, having your Little One's head in your lap becomes almost essential. Voloh's illustration shows the nanny feeding her big baby with the baby lying well across her lap. When you've become used to it, this is a somewhat intimate position that is actually very easy for you and your charge. For a big baby, however, there's no easy place to put their hands and until you're accustomed to it, this can lead to some awkward moments together. If you're worried about your big baby getting 'grabby,' you can always slip on a pair of adult baby mittens, which effectively prevent any sort of untoward behavior. If your Little One has no mittens, they can be quickly and easily ordered via online suppliers.

Be sure you've positioned your Little One as you want them and that you are both comfortable before you introduce the bottle. The first few times you try this, some squirming and shifting should be expected. Once you've found a position you like, however, you'll find that you can return to it again and again without much difficulty. Feeding an adult baby is, in this regard at least, rather like learning to ride a bicycle. Once you have mastered the technique, you don't forget it … or so I'm told.

Your big baby should need no coaxing to accept the nipple. Be aware, however, that all nipples aren't the same. As I've mentioned, some nipples are very 'slow' while others are 'fast' flow. For adult nursing, this 'flow rate' makes a big difference. Fast-flow nipples are certainly easier. After finishing a bottle with a slow flow nipple, I often feel worn out … like a pizza cook with a long-handled spatula. My tongue typically needs a day or two to recover!

Depending on the size of your Little One, you may want to stop halfway through and help your big baby burp. Or you may feel comfortable waiting until the big baby has finished the bottle. Either way, you're going to want a burp cloth of some sort across your shoulder. Bottles do leak from time to time, and burp cloths can be handy things. I once ruined a new babysitter's dress because my bottle developed a catastrophic leak early in the nursing interlude.

Almost without exceptions, babysitters have just turned me toward them and helped me sit in their lap with my chin on their shoulder. However, I'm not that big and certainly not overweight. Voloh's excellent illustration demonstrates another good burping technique: Sit your Little One astride your lap and put their chin on your shoulder. The position is identical to a hug but sitting down. The dynamics of your situation will determine what sort of position you use.

Pat the mid-back area until the baby burps. Pretty simple, right? And just like little babies, big babies will *need* to burp. Bottle feeding introduces a lot of air into the stomach, and your Little One may become downright uncomfortable if you don't offer to burp them.

An adult baby's burp isn't a loud theatrical burp. Instead, an adult's burp is often so subtle that you must strain to hear it. If I've been fed a bottle of juice, I often spit up a good bit of it. For whatever reason, my spit-up issue isn't as pronounced with soy milk or Gatorade.

Assuming you've successfully burped your big baby after about four ounces, you can settle them back into your lap and feed the other four ounces. You'll find that one hand is often holding the bottle while the other hand is supporting your Little One's head. If your hand gets tired, your big baby can always hold the bottle for a few minutes.

The lack of a free hand is one of the detriments of feeding a bottle while sitting on the sofa. If you're sitting on the floor, with your Little One's head in your lap, you have a free hand with which you can stroke their face or eyebrows. I've often fallen asleep mid-bottle while being fed on the floor. If someone falls asleep during a bottling interlude on the sofa, however, it is usually my babysitter! The actual experience is so peaceful and contenting that many of my caregivers just have not been able to stay awake. The 'ringing' sounds the bottle produces as it empties almost always rouses them.

Once the bottle is empty and you've burped your big baby, they'll likely be quite content to settle back into your lap for a brief nap. Again, this is a very peaceful and contented time, and your Little One may be battling sleep. Let them drift off for a few minutes. If you want, you can use the opportunity to check their diaper. A regressed adult baby seldom notices when they're wet. For example, I never 'know' when I 'go.' You may well find that the diaper that was bone dry when you began the nursing session is now soaked.

If you're feeding a bottle with you and the big baby on the floor, in fact, it is quite natural to check the diaper midway through the bottle and then segue to a diaper change, if that's needed. Leave your Little One holding their bottle and slide their head out of your lap. This is a good strategy for your first babysitting interlude because you're allowing your big baby to focus on finishing the bottle rather than on the diaper change. Just explain to them that you need to change their diaper and ask them to hold their bottle. You can keep up a steady monologue while you remove the wet diaper and clean up the baby. For the baby, the peaceful nursing experience continues unabated.

The 'steady monologue' I mentioned brings up a critical point. During a 'mechanical' babysitting session, if you had one, you likely interacted with your Little One as if they were an adult … albeit an adult wearing a diaper. During an actual babysitting session, on the other hand, you'll want to talk to your big baby as you would a *real* baby. Resist the temptation to talk with them as an adult! Remember that you're speaking to a toddler and gear your interaction to that level. With a little practice, you'll be able to toddler-talk your big baby while you're caring for them.

In a moment, I will share what my babysitter said to me while feeding me solid food. She has the same sort of one-sided conversation while she's bathing me, changing me, or putting me down for a nap. If you talk with your Little One as if they are an adult, they may find it difficult to regress or remain regressed. If you need to, use my babysitter's dialogue as 'patter' until you feel natural enough to create your own infantile verbiage.

Anyway: Plan to feed a couple of bottles during a typical babysitting session. A few times, I've had a babysitter feed me three bottles. Feeding an eight-ounce baby bottle typically takes about 10 to 15 minutes, whereas feeding solid food can often take half an hour or longer. Solid food is a respite of sorts from all that liquid! If done correctly, eating solid food can be one of the most babyish events your Little One gets to experience.

So, what do you feed a big baby? Unlike a 'real' baby, you can feed an adult baby practically anything. I've been fed macaroni and cheese, peanut butter and crackers, cereal, oatmeal, sandwiches, nachos – which are quite messy – and even adult frozen dinners. When I'm being babysat, I prefer being fed baby food, with some caveats.

Meat-based baby food is insipid stuff. There's no other word to describe it. Baby food with meat is genuinely awful as food for an adult. I have thrown up Gerber Macaroni and Beef. Unless you're trying to punish your big baby or just want to make a point, don't feed an adult the meat-based stuff. However, the various fruits, desserts, and vegetables aren't bad.

I typically prefer to eat almost any kind of baby food when the food itself has been well-chilled. Gerber, Beechnut, and other manufacturers still market baby desserts and strained fruits and veggies in the little glass jars – and, more recently, plastic tubs – that you can buy literally everywhere. These are cheap, easy, authentic, and typically won't induce gagging or worse. Stick with the old-line manufacturers. The boutique organic baby foods now available just don't have the same taste, and big babies can tell the difference.

Again, the venue for feeding is as important as the food itself. I have a highchair, albeit one scaled to fit an adult. The seat height is equal to the height of my washer … so some of my babysitters must stand on tiptoe to feed me. The highchair is a good bit higher than I like, but there aren't any intermediate solutions available.

The typical baby highchair always seems too small to hold an adult. Even if your big baby is very small, they're unlikely to be able to sit comfortably in a highchair made for a three-year-old. Unfortunately, adult baby highchairs are uncommon and expensive. Mine, when I purchased it years ago, was several hundred dollars. Most likely, your Little One will need to sit on a barstool or in a regular dining chair instead.

You can do a few things to make the experience more authentic, however. Use an inexpensive webbing belt with a plastic buckle to 'strap' your big baby into the chair. Unlike a real baby, your Little One is unlikely to fall out, but there's just something about the experience of being 'strapped in' that is quite childlike. Strapping an adult baby to a barstool can be a bit difficult to manage, but it can be done.

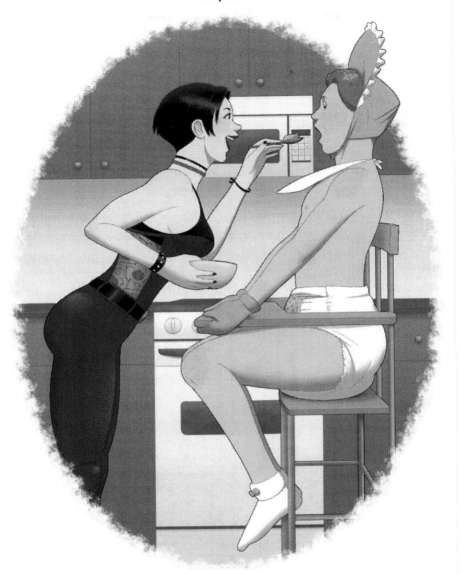

Be sure your big baby is wearing a bib. Bibbing your big baby is sound practice when you're feeding a bottle, although few babysitters have ever put bibs on me just for that. Bibs today typically don't tie around the neck. They are vastly different from the vinyl cobbler's bib I first had. Today's adult baby bibs are often specially made for Little Ones

71

and Velcro® closed. If your big baby doesn't have a bib, put one on the 'must have' list, and use a kitchen towel or hand towel, carefully tucked in around the collar of their top or diaper shirt. If you need to, use tape to secure the towel in place.

Why such concern about a bib on an adult baby? Your sole goal while feeding baby food should be to ensure that the bib *needs* to be washed! You can play all the usual games while feeding baby food ... a train going into a tunnel, an airplane coming in for a landing, a bee flying about, and so on. Done correctly, you will end your feeding time with a very messy baby!

If you're a healthcare professional, a messy feeding experience is precisely what you'd try to *avoid* when feeding an adult patient ... or a 'real' baby, usually with limited success. I've found that nurses and healthcare workers often have a difficult time managing a 'messy' feeding interlude. However, allowing your big baby to wind up smeared or streaked with baby food enhances their regressive experience. If being dressed and treated like a toddler isn't enough, mealtime is your opportunity to ensure that your Little One *looks* like a baby as well.

Some subtle hints or tips may help. If you tilt a baby spoon – or even an adult spoon – slightly, you can easily leave more food on your big baby's face than in their mouth. Use the spoon to wipe some of the food off and feed it again. The aim isn't to be neat ... in fact, the real regressive experience often comes hard on the heels of a very messy feeding. For this reason, I strongly recommend that you use an inexpensive plastic-tipped baby spoon ... or several. These are small enough that they can be easily overloaded with baby food, which makes for an enjoyable feeding experience! As you'll discover, the use of a baby spoon makes having a 'splat mat' beneath the baby's feeding chair a highly commendable prudence.

If there's some part of you that is a frustrated actor or actress, there are two elements of your big babysitting experience that allow you free rein: Feeding baby food and changing a diaper. In both cases, because you are in complete control, exaggerated motions and voice intonations are certainly allowed ... even expected. My current babysitter happily recorded what she said to me the last time she fed me in my highchair. Here's a transcript:

*Okay, open big! Here it comes!*

*No, no, you have to eat this. Open up! There you go.*

*You're going to eat this, and you're going to eat all of it.*
I'm in
*charge, and you have to do what I tell you. Open up!*

*Good boy!*

Suffice it to say that your regressed Little One may not enjoy the feeding experience quite as much as you do – I can't speak to that, because I typically cannot recall much of what was said or done beyond a vague awareness of things that happened – but as the babysitter, you can have a great deal of fun feeding a big baby. And you should!

Sippy cups are ideal for mealtime, and there's nothing special or complicated about them. Have a sippy cup filled with juice, or whatever, where your Little One can reach it. Many of my babysitters have expected me to drink from a bottle while strapped into my highchair. Sitting up makes getting liquid from a nipple a real challenge, so I prefer using a sippy cup instead.

Toddler finger foods can be fun as well, especially since they allow your big baby to practice feeding themselves. You can be as critical of their effort as you like, and some Little Ones do appear rather comical as they try to pick up small bite-sized pieces from a highchair tray. In this case, however, the aim isn't to fill the tummy but to make your Little One *feel* little. Just remember: If your regressed Little One has a 'bratty' side, toddler finger foods can become projectiles. You might want to buy your big baby that pair of baby mittens I mentioned, just to prevent such an untoward incident. In Voloh's illustration, the big baby in the highchair is wearing mittens for just this reason. Your Little One can pick up a sippy cup while wearing mittens, but not much else.

When mealtime is finished, use a clean burp cloth or several wet paper towels to clean your big baby up before you unbuckle the safety strap. Don't forget to wipe their hands, especially if you've let them indulge in finger foods.

If your Little One does have a highchair, there's nothing wrong with letting them sit in the highchair and play with a toy while you clean up. Don't forget to put their pacifier back in! Your clean-up time doesn't need to be intensive. At a minimum, however, you should deep clean the bib and highchair tray, if there is one, wipe up any spilled baby food, put the empty baby food jars in the trash, and wash the spoon you used.

# 7. | Diapers

I was about eight years old when I first discovered my mother's vintage *Better Homes and Gardens Baby Book.* The black-and-white photographs in the diapering section always fascinated me, because the mother in the pictures moved through the entire changing process with an expression that ranged from pure enjoyment to unassailable delight.

Then I watched my mother change her best friend's newborn son, and *her* expression ranged from pure enjoyment to unassailable delight. I don't recall having an experienced babysitter who was anxious or upset by the prospect of having to change me. Like feeding and burping me, changing diapers is just part of the job. However, because I have only changed my son and myself, I thought it best to complete an adult baby diaper change firsthand before I wrote this chapter.

For some prospective babysitters with healthcare training or experience, the notion of having to change an adult's diaper may induce a yawn. For other prospective babysitters, however, the idea of changing a big baby seems downright terrifying. Suffice it to say I did not find it a daunting task … and I'd never done it before. If you have any level of healthcare or childcare experience, you'll likely have no problem at all.

I grew up accustomed to wearing cloth diapers … first, the old Curity pin-on diapers and plastic pants, and then cloth diapers my mother sewed for me. Mom's more advanced versions closed with Velcro®, which was a distinct improvement over diaper pins. Pampers were just coming onto the market when I was born, and I never actually wore one until I was an undersized ten-year-old. My mom thought Pampers would be an expedient measure after a debilitating hospital stay. I don't think those early Pampers impressed either of us! On the disposable diaper front, things didn't improve much as I got older. With early adult disposable diapers, I often felt as if I were wearing a paper towel.

For years thereafter, I stuck with cloth diapers, plastic pants, and a diaper pail. As an adult, I never really wore another disposable diaper until about 2000. Even at that time, the adult disposable diapers available were either too thin or very geriatric-looking. For example, the Kendall Wings a nurse friend supplied seemed to leak without provocation.

Then, in 2006, the first couture adult baby diaper hit the market. These were Bambino Classicos, marketed via a company called, appropriately enough, Bottom Half Group. My babysitters and I loved them immediately, because they had good capacity, were cute and babyish, and didn't require laundering. The Bambino diapers launched something of a revolution. By my count, there are now nearly a hundred different diapers on the market aimed squarely at the adult baby community. Still more adult diapers are marketed in sedate colors or packaging to incontinent adults, but website content is clearly created with Little Ones clearly in mind.

I'm writing this chapter assuming that your Little One has a stash of adult baby-specific diapers on hand. If you didn't find them during your mechanical session, you should rather forcefully suggest that your baby place an order with one of the many adult diaper suppliers. Today's disposables are nothing short of wonderful, especially if you are old enough to recall the disposable desert that existed until 2006 or so.

Changing an adult's diaper is as intimate a task as changing a baby's diaper ... there's no way the process can be otherwise. As I've said before, however, the only difference is that everything is bigger ... bigger diapers, bigger changing area, bigger baby.

Beginning with your venue of choice, however, some helpful hints will make the job far easier for you to manage. I've been changed several thousand times as an adult, and from the baby's perspective, at least, I think I qualify as something of an expert.

Your first consideration is a place to change your big baby. I have a full-sized adult changing table, but few adult babies are so fortunate. Most often, you'll be making do with the bed or the floor. If the bed is soft – if the mattress is anything less than firm – then move to the floor. Or consider repurposing a folding table, coffee table, or disused dining

77

table. Just put some sort of a changing pad on top. The pad might be an adult baby-specific product, or it could be something as utilitarian as a yoga mat. For several years when I was growing up, I was changed on my old kindergarten mat.

These days, babies are typically changed wherever, whenever. I once watched my cousin change her little girl on my living room sofa. If you're going to be using a bed as a changing table, however, there's some reason for concern: A big baby weighs more, and, unlike an infant, adults tend to 'sink' into soft beds. While your Little One can lift for you and make maneuvering easier, a bed often makes securely fastening an adult diaper a tricky proposition. The amount of effort required for either bed or floor is about the same, but you'll find that you can vastly improve the fit of the diaper if you use the firmest surface available.

In a typical four-hour babysitting session, you will be changing three or four diapers. Usually, you'll want to plan for a diaper change following a bottle, following any lengthy period of sedentary activity, like watching television, and after a nap.

With this sort of constant repetition in mind, you'll do well to create a 'changing station' on the floor, bed, or table you've chosen. When you have the arrangement of essential items as you want it, take a photo with your cellphone, and ask your Little One to recreate the space for you ahead of each subsequent babysitting session.

Looking on and beneath my changing table, here's what you'd find:

- A dinosaur motif adult changing pad, like a bed pad
- A stack of a half-dozen disposable diapers
- A package of baby wipes
- A tube of Desitin®
- Baby Magic lotion
- Johnson's Cornstarch baby powder
- A couple of burp cloths

- A roll of diaper disposal bags

- A small toy and an extra pacifier

Some of the items on the list demand an explanation. The small diaper disposal bags, available at Target and other retailers, will accommodate a rolled adult disposable diaper. These can substitute for a diaper pail, allowing you to take a pleasantly scented wrapped bundle to the trash after each diaper change.

The small toy – in my case, a miniature double-decker bus – is obviously for me. This is just something to occupy my hands while my babysitter does her thing.

I very seldom require Desitin®, but it's helpful to have it when it is needed.

A word of advice: Don't bother asking your Little One if they need to be changed. When we're regressed, we typically know about as much as you do on the subject! When in doubt, do a quick diaper check and see for yourself. If the diaper feels as if your big baby might be a quart or two low, that's likely the case.

Tell your big baby that it's time to change their diaper. I must climb onto my changing table, but your Little One will most likely lie down on the floor or bed. Hand them something to play with and make sure their pacifier is in place. Then start by removing any extraneous clothing ... pajama bottoms, shorts, skirt, and so on. If your Little One is wearing a onesie, unsnap the snaps and fold the back flap well underneath them for safekeeping. There's really no need to remove a diaper shirt, mittens, booties, or a bonnet. You can just keep them in place.

The diaper will likely be held in place by two tape or Velcro® tabs on each side. A few adult baby diapers try to mimic Pampers and have only a single tape per side, but these haven't really caught on because they are exceptionally difficult to fit properly. The one-tape design works well on babies and toddlers. Unfortunately, most adults are just too large for one tape to cover all that real estate.

Pull the tape tabs away and lower the front of the diaper to inspect what diaper manufacturers call 'the insult.' With the diaper still in place beneath your Little One, use baby wipes to clean them up ... both in front and underneath. Unlike the cloth diapers of days gone by, disposable diapers tend to wick urine away from the skin and disperse it all over, and you'll need to be sure your big baby is clean. This will require some effort and two or three baby wipes. Of course, your baby can lift their hips, which is decidedly helpful when you're cleaning their bottom.

One of my babysitters was in the habit of 'waving' baby wipes above me, thinking that cleaning me was a minor matter. She was squeamish about touching me. But cleaning isn't an unimportant task, and you should wipe like you mean business. If you don't think baby wipes are doing the job, get up and get a warm wet washcloth. If you're up to the task of changing the diaper, you shouldn't 'wimp out' on the cleanup just because you're afraid to touch your Little One in an intimate area. If you fail to clean thoroughly enough, you'll have to remedy the situation while your big baby is in the bathtub. You can have them stand up in the bathtub so you can wash them front and back, but cleaning at each diaper change is easier all the way around.

Once your big baby is clean, you're through with the old diaper. Pull the used diaper from beneath your Little One, drop the used baby wipes into the middle, and roll it up. Use the tape tabs to seal the bundle shut, then tuck the used diaper into a diaper disposal bag or put it in a nearby diaper pail.

Unfold a fresh diaper all the way and use your fingers to crease it down the entire middle. Run a finger inside each leg gather to ensure the gather is standing up. This is called 'fluffing,' and it is necessary because of the way diaper manufacturers pack so many adult diapers into small bags or boxes. Ask the Little One to lift their hips, then slide the 'fluffed' diaper beneath your big baby. As you do so, double-check to be sure the tape tabs are at the back. The top of the diaper's back waistband should be centered beneath your baby's waist.

Have your Little One lower their hips onto the diaper just to be sure it is positioned correctly. Squirt a dollop of baby lotion into the palm of your hand, and warm it a bit by rubbing your hands together. Then, apply the lotion to your baby's diaper area ... front and back. The idea is to create a moisture barrier of sorts, so two liberal squirts of lotion may be required. If you have powder on hand, sprinkle it atop the area you've coated with lotion ... not so much for the absorbent properties, but because the smell and sight of lingering powder are regression triggers for most big babies.

Now, use a burp cloth or a baby wipe to wipe off your fingers. Any lingering lotion or powder will create quite a problem when you try to tape an adult diaper closed. If you get lotion or powder on sticky tapes, they won't stick well … or at all.

Bring the front of the diaper up between your Little One's legs. Tug up firmly on the top of the front of the diaper to seat the leg gathers, then smooth the front along your big baby's tummy. Put one palm firmly on one side to keep it in place, then bring the back wing – and the tapes – over that side of the front of the diaper. Fasten the bottom tape first, then move to the top. When you've finished that side, repeat the same process with the other side. Many of today's adult baby diapers have Velcro® tabs that allow you to reposition them until you get the fit exactly as you want it. If the tabs are tapes, however, be prepared to tug them back off and then carefully reseal them.

Once the diaper is as secure as you want it to be, you've completed the changing process. Help your big baby up from the changing pad, then clean off any extraneous powder from the mat and dispose of the used diaper. One of my babysitters always gave me a playful swat on my diapered bottom as I got up, just as a reward for lying still for five minutes. I always thought that gesture was shortsighted on her part!

I've never actually changed an adult cloth diaper, but since I wore them for many years, I can tell you that about the only thing different in the process is that you'll have to remove plastic pants first, and the cleaning process is somewhat different. That's because cloth diapers absorb in a very specialized area ... in the front for boys, and in the middle for girls. If your big baby uses the large prefold cloth diapers with pins, be sure to practice during your introductory mechanical session to ensure you don't stick them! My mom was motivated to try Velcro® on the cloth diapers she made me because she stuck me with a diaper pin that went both in and out!

Incidentally, there are a wide variety of cloth diapers available today with Velcro® closures or snaps, so if you're uncomfortable using diaper pins, suggest to your Little One that they upgrade their stash. Big babies typically refer to diapers and baby things they have hidden away as a 'stash.' This isn't a drug-related term.

I still have a dozen or so adult pocket diapers like the ones Zoey used when she babysat me back in 2007. Pocket diapers are quite discrete and, because they usually snap rather than pin, they are far easier to change than cloth prefold diapers. However, if I'm not changed every hour or so, the pocket diapers tend to leak. The inserts, which slip into a pocket inside the diaper, are just not capable of absorbing what I can dish out. Accordingly, I much prefer disposable diapers, which hold five times as much comfortably and without leaking.

You may have nursery music playing away during your diaper changes, but you'll need to insert a monologue of your own as well.

83

Don't be afraid to say something like, "Let's see what you did," or "Good job!" as you pull open the diaper. Of course, caregivers and patients in a healthcare setting would be mortified by such comments, but a big baby will expect them.

I asked my current babysitter to record herself getting me up from a nap and changing my diaper. Here's a transcript of what she said to me:

*Wake up! Wake up! Hello!*

*Did you sleep good? Yeah?*

*Let's get you out of the crib and get you out of that wet diapee.*

*Can you get out on your own? You need help? Let nanny help you.*

*There you go. Let's go over and change your diapee.*

*Oh, my goodness! This thing is soaked!*

*I'll bet you're glad to get out of this.*

*Let's get you cleaned up. This might be a little cold.*

*All clean! Lift up for nanny, please.*

*You like the lotion, don't you? Now, some powder. Tickle, tickle!*

*Let me throw this away. This is a heavy diaper!*

*You want a hug? You're still sleepy, huh? How about we get a snack?*

*Take my hand and let's go to the kitchen.*

I know the lack of context makes this example difficult to judge or emulate, but you get the idea. Don't be afraid to interact with your Little One as if they really are two years old.

Over the past half-century, I've only had one babysitter tell me that she looked forward to changing a dirty diaper, and I cannot imagine many caregivers like that task very much. However, unless you provoke my digestive tract by feeding me something that has a laxative effect, I'm generally only wet. Unfortunately, dirty diapers are occasionally a part of the job. Because I'm regressed, I don't "know" when I "go," and a diaper that is more than wet is always a possibility. I had one babysitter care for me nearly every week for almost four years, and in all that time, she changed *three* dirty diapers.

I've had healthcare professionals who took time to 'glove up' at each diaper change on the off chance that they'd have to deal with a dirty diaper. That's fine, of course, but the dirty diaper was typically never an issue to begin with. As an adult baby myself, I guess all I can say is this: A big baby's bowel movement isn't radioactive waste. It's just ... *poop.* If you're a prospective babysitter and assuming your Little One seems healthy and well, you shouldn't let the prospect of having to change a dirty diaper dissuade you from taking the job.

I'm a psychological infantilist, but even so, I'm an adult male. If you rub hard enough or long enough in the right places, I get hard. Unbelievably, I also get an erection when I am cold, which means I'm 'wired' differently than most men. If you're changing a diaper and your big baby gets hard, just ignore it. Trust me when I tell you that your Little One will likely want you to do that! None of us enjoys the fact that a certain part of our anatomy wants 'adult' attention when the rest of us craves exactly the opposite.

Finally, I've had a couple of babysitter candidates who didn't want to change diapers at all. These ladies tactfully suggest that I wear training pants instead. While I do have training pants, I usually cannot regress while wearing them ... I'm too focused on keeping the furniture from getting wet! A diaper is elemental to big baby regression, and your Little One will, to a certain extent, be depending on your ability to diaper and change them.

# 8. | Bathing

E ven if you're not an infantilist, you probably enjoy a warm, relaxing bubble bath. If you're on the other side of the bathtub, however, bathing an adult baby can be an intricate process. The aim of this chapter is to make that process an easily manageable one … something that will calm and soothe you and your Little One as well.

For starters, recognize that there's nothing particularly high-tech about a bubble bath. In many respects, what you're providing for your big baby is as old-fashioned as it gets … a parental ritual so ancient that its roots are lost in the mists of time. If that very thought doesn't bring you a sense of wonder and awe, it should!

Your first concern is safety. Each year, an incredible number of accidents befall adults in bathrooms. Your Little One must be able to climb into the bathtub and to get back out on their own.

If you're not certain your big baby can get out of a bathtub, don't get them into it!

I have fallen twice in bathtubs, and, while I'm hardly athletic, I am in very good shape. Accidents can happen … and will, given the opportunity! Don't let your Little One try to stand up in the bathtub without having you on hand to help them. Have your arm around their torso to ensure that they do not fall.

Three types of liquids are required for bathing an adult baby:

• Copious amounts of water

• Bubble bath, and

• Baby wash

There's quite a difference between baby wash and bubble bath. The bubble bath generates bubbles but doesn't do much more. The baby wash, on the other hand, strips dirt and oils from your Little One's skin and gets them clean. If you rely on the bubble bath as a washing agent, I imagine you'll find it woefully inefficient.

For the bath itself, I'd also recommend that you have on hand:

- A bath mitt
- A rinse cup
- Bath toys
- A bath sheet or large towel

The bath mitt allows you to scrub your big baby without fear of scratching with your nails or worrying about overly intimate contact. I've had the same bath mitt for a decade or so. These are tough little terrycloth gloves designed to do a specific job. If you wash it after each bathing interlude, you should be able to reuse the same one for some time.

The babyish bath mitts are becoming hard to find and can usually only be bought as a four-pack.

A rinse cup is just a large plastic cup, and you use it when you're rinsing the baby wash lather from your Little One. You'll find a rinse cup especially handy if you decide to wash your baby's hair. You can use an ordinary plastic kitchen cup since there's nothing inherently special required. I've had mine since I was a 'real' little kid.

During your mechanical session, you may have noted a lack of bath supplies or bath toys. If that's the case, there's no reason why you shouldn't arrange a shopping expedition with your big baby. Certain items – like baby wash and a bath mitt – are essentials, but your Little One can select the rest.

Since I've been at this awhile, I could probably write a book on the topic of bath toys. Instead, I'll just cut to the chase, because over the years, I have found only three or four that help me stay regressed. The rest, particularly those that need suction cups to attach to the bathtub, are simply more trouble than they are worth.

I have a set of stacking cups, which nest to form a small bundle when I'm not being bathed. Each cup has openings in the bottom to allow it to drain, and I have a lot of fun filling and emptying them. I also have a magnetic toy fishing pole and three or four magnetic 'bobbers' that sit atop the water waiting for me to 'catch' them. I have a set of bath crayons around somewhere, but I seldom use them because the cleanup can be rather arduous. Finally, I have the rather ubiquitous rubber duck.

Be sure to start filling the bathtub *before* you begin to undress your Little One. I'd recommend that you let your Little One play elsewhere while you start the bath, and then bring them into the bathroom when the tub is about halfway full. Be sure to add copious amounts of bubble bath to warm water. Bring your big baby in and stand them on the bathmat. You can sit on the closed toilet and undress them down to their diaper. Leave their pacifier in place throughout the bath

89

and the nap or playtime interlude that follows. I think one of the reasons I enjoy bath time so much is that I never have to speak a word.

Years ago, one of my babysitters was a pediatric Nurse Practitioner. We'd known each other for many years. As she undressed me, she'd tell me silly stories about buttons refusing to unbutton and zippers getting stuck. Before I knew it, I'd be standing on the bathmat clad only in a wet diaper. I always appreciated the way she distracted me with her monologue so I would not be inordinately self-conscious. Once I was in the bath and she was bathing me, she'd pour cup after cup of warm water on my chest. When I closed my eyes, at her suggestion, I almost felt as if I were floating. The experience was among the most peaceful I've ever had. I think only parasailing has been more sublime.

If your Little One is wearing a disposable diaper, you can just remove it while they're standing there. Hold onto the back while you pull away the tape tabs. If the diaper is just wet, you can let the front drop, then cup it in your hand and roll the whole thing away from the big baby. Some cloth diapers – like my snap-on pocket diapers – can be easily removed while standing as well. If your big baby is wearing a cloth diaper and plastic pants, however, you might do well to have them lie on the bathmat so you can pull down the plastic pants and remove the diaper.

A few babysitters have wiped me off with a baby wipe before I stepped into the bathtub, but this is usually unnecessary. I say 'usually' because I'm seldom more than very wet. If you've already had to change a dirty diaper, however, you might want to take a baby wipe and wipe that bottom thoroughly before allowing your Little One into the bathtub.

Typically, the bath itself is a three-step process:

- Soaking
- Playing while you wash
- Rinsing

Again, if you're planning to leave the bathroom for any reason, you should admonish your big baby not to try to stand up in the bathtub while you're gone.

I guess I should mention that I have talked with experienced 'professional' babysitters who have stepped away for a few moments and come back to find the bathroom an absolute disaster area! Big babies love to splash, and things can get very wet in a hurry. If this is your first time bathing an adult baby, you might want to mention that excessive splashing is an offense punishable by a lengthy time-out. Usually, that's all the warning your Little One will require. When I was still quite young, my babysitter told me that if I splashed, she'd paddle me into tomorrow. While rather harsh, this little injunction certainly got my attention. She and the bathroom emerged unscathed, and I never deliberately splashed her while she was bathing me.

Let your Little One soak for a few minutes. Use the time to go find the clothes in which you'll dress your big baby after the bath is complete. Or, if you're going to re-dress the baby in the same clothes they were wearing, pick these up from the bathroom and fold them neatly, then put them somewhere you can easily find them when the bath is finished.

The time I spend soaking is always a placid interlude. I don't do much playing with bath toys until my babysitter returns. Warm water genuinely *feels* good, and I like to prolong soaks for as long as I can. I quite often emerge from an overlong bath looking much like a prune!

Once you are back alongside the bathtub, how do you wash? The process isn't unlike bathing a 'real' baby. Use your bath mitt and some baby wash to work up a good lather on the chest, arms, and legs, then carefully wash your big baby's face. Wash hands and feet, then give the genitals a quick swipe. Usually, that's all that's required. You can certainly ask your baby to kneel in the bathtub if you think their genitals or backside need more attention, but usually, that's not necessary.

While you can bathe an adult in four or five minutes, you'll want to take your time. There's a reason for this: Your big baby will want to play. Be sure their bath toys are close at hand and let them play while you wash them.

If you decide you want to wash your Little One's hair – and you do not have to – you should provide them a washcloth or something with which to cover their eyes. Even 'tearless' baby shampoos induce tears, especially in adults with sensitive eyes. I've had several operations on my eyes and washing my hair without helping me avoid getting soap in them is a perilous business. For that reason, most of my babysitters have used baby wash and handed me a washcloth before they started on my hair. Quite often, however, they choose not to wash my hair at all.

Use the rinse cup to rinse the hair, then rinse your big kid from head to toe. If you've done it right, you'll pull the drain plug about the time your Little One has been in the bath for about half an hour. For safety, let the water drain until there's only an inch or so in the bottom of the tub, then help your big baby stand up. Once they're securely on their feet, grab your bath sheet and begin drying them from the hair or face down. Like drying a 'real' baby, you'll want to make sure you have dried all the creases, folds, and places in between.

The bathtub should be completely drained by the time you finish drying. Wrap your baby in the towel, then help them step carefully out of the tub. Have them stand on the bathmat while you make sure they're dry. Don't be afraid to retrieve the bath towel and finish drying if further drying is necessary. Most often, I have a foot or something that is still wet, and my babysitter has to dry that area before the bath really comes to a close.

Like their smaller counterparts, big babies tend to get chilly easily. However, dressing a Little One while they stand on the bathmat is a genuine challenge. You're far better off to walk them back into their bedroom and have them lie on the bed or floor. Retrieve the clothing you selected while they were soaking in the bathtub and dress them quickly, but carefully. You can put on a diaper in about 30 seconds if your moves are practiced, and pajamas or a onesie are easily slipped on as well.

While you're dressing your Little One, pay some attention to how animated they seem to be. I'm almost always ready for a nap after a bath. If you choose to put your big baby down for a few minutes, you may find that they drift off quite quickly and stay asleep for 15 or 20 minutes.

You can do all this with a minimum of monologue. Just tell your baby what you're doing as you dress them, then help them to bed and tuck them in. You may want to read a very quick story as the Little One drifts off, but that's often not necessary.

If, on the other hand, you decide to involve your Little One in a playtime after the bath, choose an activity that is somewhat languid in nature. Don't expect them to play a board game or even color in a coloring book. Find an activity that suits a relaxed, almost tired mood.

Once your Little One is napping or playing contentedly, go back to the bathroom and clean up. Put the wet bath towel in the hamper, rinse out the bathtub, and be sure all the bath toys, baby wash, shampoo, and the bath mitt are accounted for. Most of my babysitters have left the bath mitt and toys on the side of the bathtub to dry, which is always very helpful.

Done correctly, giving a big baby a bath is a peaceful, almost calming interlude in the middle of your time together. As an infantilist, I look forward to baths perhaps more than I anticipate any other element of a babysitting session. If you spend the time necessary to hone your bathing skills, you'll find that the contentment you can deliver with a bubble bath will be a genuine benefit for your Little One.

# 9. | Final Notes

**C**aring for an adult baby isn't particularly glamorous, and most of the time, the activity itself is hidden from view. But there's one word to describe your Little One's perspective on the few hours of your time that you offer: **Priceless.**

While every session is different, and each will be exciting for your big baby in a unique way, caregivers can become a bit bored with the standard babysitting scenario. In this final chapter, I'll offer up some ideas for making your babysitting time extraordinary ... and how, if you find that you enjoy the work, you can expand the services you offer to encompass more adult babies.

Once you and your Little One have settled into something approaching a routine, there's nothing wrong with packing a diaper bag and taking your big baby on what I euphemistically refer to as a 'field trip' ... out of the house. You can go to the park and play on the swings, go to the zoo, go shopping for new bath toys or coloring books, or even go to a fair, a flea market or a mall. There are but four things to keep in mind:

**First, it's probably not wise to let everyone in on your 'little secret.'** As a rule, I avoid exposing unaware and non-consenting people to my infantilism. My babysitters and I do go outside while I'm wearing diapers and baby clothes beneath my street clothes, but we don't call attention to the fact or advertise it in any way. Doing so would be spectacularly unfair to others and would likely result in just the sort of adverse attention I typically work to avoid.

Don't take your Little One into a store or public place and baby-talk them, but don't try to make them 'adult' while you're out and about. The compromise you'll need to make is a sort of limited communication that allows your big baby to continue to feel as if they *belong* in that hidden diaper. You can use exaggerated excitement when you see something interesting or find something to buy but keep the volume low and unobtrusive. This process requires some thought and prearrangement on your part, but your Little One will appreciate the effort and enjoy the result.

**Second, clothing and diaper changes can be problematic.** While malls and larger stores – like Target in the United States – often have family restrooms, many smaller venues do not. If you and your Little One are of the same sex, this isn't as big a challenge as it is if you're not, since you can often go into the same restroom and use a stall to change. For mixed-gender couples, however, a family restroom is essential. I do a good deal of fact-finding ahead of time to ensure that anywhere my babysitter wants to take me has this sort of convenience. If there isn't a suitable restroom, we can typically find one close enough to allow us to make the trip.

Changing a diaper in a family restroom is an art unto itself. Typically, I'm changed while I'm standing, since the changing table is usually designed for much smaller babies. I have, in a few cases, been able to use a very sturdy built-in changing table, but the proportions tend to be a bit cramped.

The key to changing your big baby while they are standing is to ensure that you change them before they're about to float away. A very wet diaper makes for an exponentially more difficult change. Your Little One can hold onto the back of the diaper as you pull away the tapes. When you are putting on a clean diaper, use the pressure between the big baby and the wall to hold the fresh diaper in place as you pull it up between their legs.

**Third, you'll need to be prepared.** A diaper bag or backpack typically doesn't hold a lot, but it holds enough ... if you pack it properly. Unless it's Halloween, you can leave the pacifiers, bottles, bibs, and baby food at home.

Focus instead on carrying with you a couple of diapers, a small package of wipes, and a change of clothing ... a clean t-shirt or something. Accidents happen, especially with adult babies.

**Fourth, your Little One will likely be self-conscious.** Those of us who wear adult diapers in a 'recreational' way often worry about whether other people can tell. Usually, of course, other people don't notice. You'll want to continually reassure your big baby that no one can tell what's beneath their skirt, pants, or shorts. The goal of the 'field trip' is to add a little interest or excitement to an otherwise routine babysitting progression … not to provoke additional anxiety.

When I'm out and about with a babysitter, I always let her drive. Of course, I also reimburse her for gasoline and any admission fees or other associated expenses. If I know we're going shopping or stopping for a meal, I give my babysitter my credit card and let her pay. The last thing I want to do, as she knows, is to be forced to interact like an adult in some way. I usually order for myself if we're in a restaurant, but the rest of the time, I'm a bashful, shy, non-verbal little kid.

Years ago, my babysitters used my minivan to take me out, and we went to lunch, shopping, and so on. I sat in the passenger seat and the babysitter drove. The beauty of the minivan was that we didn't have to worry about family restrooms, which weren't as plentiful back then. Instead, the van had tinted windows and a back seat that was removable. Babysitters could lay me down in the back and change me when required. Diaper changes weren't particularly pleasant when the weather was overly hot, but at least they were possible.

The only issue you'll encounter these days is when there's a queue for a family restroom. You'll have to wait your turn like everyone else. Just try to be prepared for some stares when you and your big baby emerge. As a courtesy, you shouldn't monopolize family restrooms in any way. Be mindful that there are overstressed parents and caregivers wanting to use the same facility, so some degree of efficiency is always called for.

Adult babies are often myopically focused on the care they're receiving. This is probably as it should be … when we're not being babysat, we are often shopping for diapers or baby things online, reading adult baby fiction, or posting to any of several internet bulletin boards created exclusively for infantilists. I say all that to say this: The big baby for whom you provide care will often have an entire list of things you can try during a babysitting interlude. Just ask!

You'll have ideas as well, and it's often a good notion to plan an 'adult' lunch or coffee with your big baby and meet as adults to share your thoughts. Over the years, I've had babysitters suggest a few things that raised eyebrows. For example, one babysitter wanted me to deliberately misbehave so she could spank me, another wanted to dress me "all in pink, like a little girl," and one young woman wanted, unusually enough, for me to cry while she changed me, as a 'real' infant would. Although I've never been hauled across someone's knee and spanked as an adult baby, I've generally been happy to accommodate any request a caregiver made.

Finally, let's take a bit of a mental leap. Some of my caregivers have told me after the first session or two that adult babysitting just seemed to suit them. These women were usually somewhat older, more maternal 'empty nesters' who missed the bonding and intimacy of caring for a baby or toddler and wanted it back ... albeit on an occasional basis. Quite a few had a need for the additional income, and since big babysitting tends to pay more than conventional babysitting, they were looking for opportunities to expand their adult baby client base.

If you find yourself dealing with the same sort of emotions after your first babysitting forays, just know that there is an entire universe of Little Ones out there desperate for your care. Your initial adult baby client may be able to refer you to other big babies in your immediate area. Beyond that, the internet awaits! You'll find several internet messaging boards on which you can post notices.

Writing a good initial advertisement is a genuine art. You'll need to be clear on several points. First, if you have no way to babysit in your own home, you'll have to mention that your caregiving services are outcall only. If you have specific time windows when you're available, mention them as well. Also, mention your hourly fee. Across the United States, fees for outcall adult babysitters can range from $25 to $100 an hour or more.

If you choose to invest in a nursery full of adult baby furniture and provide all the diapers and other needed supplies as well, you can charge several times that amount and offer sitting on an in-call basis.

Perhaps you don't want to take your Little One on a 'field trip,' or you don't want to change dirty diapers. Mention any stipulations and include some information about yourself. Ask your big baby to help you create a 'living biography' that accurately describes your babysitting style, attributes, and appearance.

Once you've posted on several adult baby boards, stand back! Such postings will generate a lot of attention, and you'll typically have overflowing email as a result.

As I mentioned at the outset, adult babysitting is a brave new world for those ready to embrace the sheer joy of providing tender loving care to Little Ones who are starved for the experience. Be passionate about what you do ... and have fun!

# Acknowledgements

Grateful appreciation to Rosalie Bent for her keen insight and practical guidance.

Thanks to all my friends on ADISC.org – the Adult Baby/Diaper Lover/Incontinence Support Community – for ideas and assistance. Special thanks to LilBabyJooce for her invaluable information on clothing for adult baby girls.

Heartfelt thanks to many of my former caregivers who contributed to the various chapters or reviewed the book as it was being written. To Anita, thanks for reminding me that even changing a dirty diaper can be a joyful and giving act. To Jan and Jos, thanks for keeping me focused on the prime directive of big babysitting, which is having fun! Zoey, Lisa, and Pat earned my appreciation for their 'mechanical session' guidance. Sandy offered playlist tips and dialogue recordings, and Susan provided much of the impetus necessary to write the book. I wager she'll be among the first to read it! Susan has always loved me for who I am, and that includes being a messy toddler at times. I have a new appreciation for the freedom such unconditional love can bring.

I also have new appreciation for Voloh's talent and illustrations and have found in him a kindred spirit of sorts. We already plan to work together again.

Finally, thanks to those readers of *Sitter Search* who suggested this additional book.

*– Sam McCue*